'WELL DONE, BOYS'

'WELL DONE, BOYS'

The life and crimes of Robert Black

Robert Church

Foreword by

The Honourable Lord Cowie

Constable · London

First published in Great Britain 1996
by Constable & Company Ltd
3 The Lanchesters, 162 Fulham Palace Road
London W6 9ER
Copyright © 1996 by Robert Church
The right of Robert Church to be identified
as the author of this work has been asserted
by him in accordance with the Copyright,
Designs and Patents Act 1988

Set in Monophoto Sabon 11pt by
Servis Filmsetting Ltd, Manchester
Printed and bound in Great Britain by
Hartnolls Ltd, Bodmin

ISBN 0 09 474150 6

A CIP catalogue record for this book
is available from the British Library

Also by Robert Church

Murder in East Anglia
Accidents of murder
More murder in East Anglia
Anglian blood (Co-editor)

To all those who for so long sought Robert Black

Rachel weeping for her children, and would not be comforted, because they are not.

St Matthew 2: 18

CONTENTS

ILLUSTRATIONS

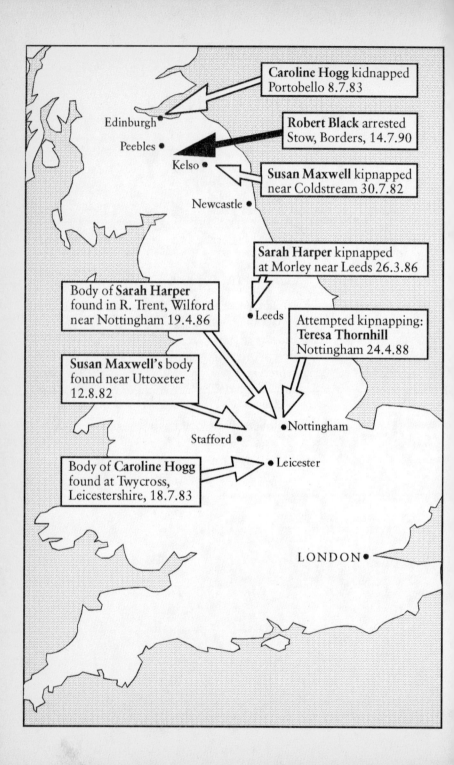

AUTHOR'S NOTE

This story of Robert Black and his crimes has been written following extensive research and many interviews. Where I have been unable to unravel to my complete satisfaction the exact sequence of events, or to determine the thoughts and reactions of people to those events, I have deduced these from the available evidence and from my observation and knowledge of the individuals concerned.

This device has been resorted to only rarely, and has been adopted to avoid ambiguity, and to prevent interruption in the flow of the narrative.

Any factual error, misrepresentation or misinterpretation is therefore solely my responsibility and should not be attributed to any individuals mentioned in the book.

R.C.

ACKNOWLEDGEMENTS

Many people from a variety of sources have helped during the research for this book. Several have most generously provided hospitality when I have visited them personally, and all have been unfailingly helpful and courteous when replying to my letters and answering my questions. To each one of them I extend my sincere thanks.

A number of people whom I have seen, or with whom I have corresponded, have assisted me on condition that they remain anonymous or adopt a pseudonym. I have, of course, agreed with this proviso.

My gratitude and appreciation go to The Honourable Lord Cowie for writing the Foreword to this book.

The individuals and organisations named below are not shown in order of priority.

Tony Bailey, London; John Banks, London; Ms Dawn Skinner, London; George Head, London; Stanley Ottoway, London; Trevor Rigby, London; Mrs Geraldine Jones, London; John Newton, London; Jimmy Wallace, Fort William; Andrew Wells, Grangemouth; Brian Kirby, Grangemouth; Mrs Anne McKenzie, Coldstream; Mrs Sylvia Fletcher, Coldstream; Michael Fletcher, Coldstream; Mrs Marion Rogers, Portobello; Paul Sapwell, Edinburgh; Fergus Campbell, Edinburgh; John Hope, Morley; Mrs Lynne Owen, Morley; George Jackson, Morley; John Barnett, Nottingham; Robert Braithwaite, Galashiels; Angus Proctor, Galashiels; Mrs Jennifer Booth, Portobello; James McKenzie, Newcastle; John Stanhope, Manchester; Henk van Dijk, Amsterdam.

Hector Clark, Deputy Chief Constable (Ret'd), Lothian and Borders Police; Thomas Wood, Assistant Chief Constable, L & B; Roger Orr, Detective Chief Inspector, L & B; Andrew Brown, Assistant Chief Constable, L & B; Dennis Cleugh, Detective Chief Inspector, L & B;

[13]

Lindsey McBride, Detective Constable, L & B; Alan Cossar, Detective
Constable, L & B; Tom Bell, Detective Constable, L & B; Peter Herward,
Superintendent, Staffordshire Police; Brian Luton, Detective Constable,
Staffs; Tony Beardmore, Detective Constable, Staffs; Tony Leighton,
Detective Constable, Staffs; John Stainthorpe, Detective Superintendent,
West Yorkshire Police; M. Woodhouse, Detective Chief Superintendent,
W. Yorks; M.J. Perry, Acting Assistant Chief Constable, Leicestershire
Constabulary.

Richard Wood, *Burton Mail*; Roger Burrell, Assistant Editor,
Newcastle Evening Chronicle; Miss Evelyn Ainsley, *Newcastle Evening
Chronicle*; Judy Kingscott and the staff of the Local Studies Library,
Nottingham; Mrs Barbara Heathcote, Local Studies Librarian,
Newcastle upon Tyne Central Library; Maria Hoy, Local Studies Library,
Newcastle upon Tyne Central Library; Mrs M. Doneghy, Visitor Centre,
Kinlochleven; Mrs Anne McQueen, Chief Librarian, Yorkshire Post
Newspapers; staff of Local History Library, Leeds; Mrs M. Sharp, Local
Studies Library, Edinburgh City Library; Chrissie Smith, Librarian,
Derby Evening Telegraph; J.L. Harpham Ltd, Official Court Reporters,
Newcastle upon Tyne; J.C. Shaw, Chief Clerk, Newcastle upon Tyne Law
Courts; Peter Chapman, Chief Librarian, The Scotsman Publications
Ltd; the staff of the British Museum newspaper library; Don Short, my
agent at Solo Syndication and Literary Agency, London; Miles
Huddleston, Director, Constable Publishers.

In addition contemporaneous reports from the following newspapers
supplemented other research: *Nottingham Evening Post*; *Derby Evening
Telegraph*; *Burton Mail*; *Yorkshire Evening Post*; *Newcastle Evening
Chronicle*; *The Scotsman*; *Newcastle Journal*; *The Times*; *The Guardian*;
The Independent; *Daily Mail*; *Daily Mirror*.

Finally, my wife Dorothy, without whose encouragement and support
this project would not have been completed.

FOREWORD

The murder of a young child in the course of a sexual assault is, arguably, the most heinous and despicable offence of which man is capable. It is universally condemned, and even the most hardened criminals are not slow to express their disgust at such behaviour, labelling the perpetrators 'beasts' and causing the prison authorities to segregate them in secure accommodation for their own protection.

It is not surprising therefore that Robert Black, who committed three such murders and abducted a fourth young girl with probably the same intention, is regarded with such revulsion in all sections of the community. His behaviour was beyond belief and, no doubt in the minds of many, beyond redemption.

In these circumstances Mr Church is to be commended for the objective and restrained account which he gives of the life and activities of Robert Black. He could, as so often happens nowadays, have descended into the depths of sensationalism and dwelt on the more lurid aspects of Black's behaviour but to his great credit he has concentrated on the factual aspects of the case, and, to my mind, that only goes to enhance the quality of his work and to emphasise its integrity.

In this absorbing book, there are many facets upon which I would like to have commented, but space does not permit. Accordingly, as a judge and especially as a Scottish judge I have selected three points which are of particular interest to me but also I hope of general importance as well.

The first is the part played by the police in this investigation. In describing the monumental task which faced them in bringing Black to justice, Mr Church has brought to our attention the dedication and perseverance of a body of men who never wavered in their determination to solve what was at first a single crime and ended up as four, and at the same time managed to deal tactfully and sympathetically with the grieving parents.

In this day and age much criticism is directed against the police, no doubt some of it justifiably, but this investigation showed how much the public is indebted to their consummate professionalism. The inquiries which they carried out were painstaking and thorough and involved not only the examination of numerous documents, but the interviewing of many thousands of people. It is often forgotten that the evidence which is led in court is only a fraction of the work which the police have carried out, and this case was a good example of that situation. The only comparison which I would make with the herculean task which the police undertook and completed is the extent of the research which Mr Church himself must have carried out to bring this aspect of the case to our notice.

The second point is the prominence which Mr Church has given to the feelings and reactions of the families of the young victims of these offences. I have already made reference to the manner in which the police appear to have acted, but it is only in comparatively recent times that the consequences of crime on those who are directly affected have been recognised by the law, and attempts made to mitigate them. It is particularly important that this should be done in cases where parents have been devastated by the loss of a child in criminal circumstances, and so I was pleased to see that Mr Church had devoted a lot of space to the reactions of the families of these children and has made their views known.

The third and final facet of this book upon which I would like to comment is perhaps more controversial, but is of particular interest to me, and that is the description of the legal process which brought Robert Black to trial and culminated in his conviction.

I have to say at the outset that it is with some trepidation that I embark on a discussion of these matters since, as a Scottish judge, I am obviously not as familiar with the English criminal law and procedure as I might be. However, having said that, there are some aspects of this case to which I must draw attention as being different from the Scottish system, and which might have brought about a different result had proceedings been taken in Scotland.

I should say straight away, on the one hand, that I am entirely satisfied that the case against Robert Black should have been brought in England, and I welcome the outcome. There was every reason to believe that, apart from the abduction of Caroline Hogg in Portobello, the probabilities are that all the other offences were committed in England, and the Crown Office in Edinburgh was fully justified not only in deciding not to take proceedings in Scotland for that abduction becuase of the paucity of the evidence, but also in not objecting to proceedings on the remaining offences being taken in England – if indeed it was consulted. On the other hand I am bound to say that if Black had been tried under Scottish procedure, there is a possibility that he might have been acquitted by a Not Proven verdict. Of course, I am speculating on this point, because I am not aware of the full extent of the evidence which was led at Newcastle, but I have a feeling that such circumstantial evidence as would have been admissible under Scottish procedure might not have been enough in the hands of a competent defence advocate to persuade a jury beyond reasonable doubt that Black had committed these offences. Certainly there was evidence of his sexual deviation involving young girls. There was also a great deal of evidence which put him in the vicinity of the initial abduction of each of these children, but at the end of the day I cannot help feeling that what must have swayed the jury in this case was the evidence of the abduction of Mandy Wilson in Stow and Black's conviction for that offence. That was the one aspect of the evidence which bore directly on the circumstances of the other offences as being similar in its facts, and, in my opinion, that evidence would not have been allowed under our procedure, leaving only the other circumstantial evidence for the jury to consider.

In our Scottish system of law it is not permitted to lead evidence of a crime with which the accused is not charged, i.e. which does not appear on the particular indictment with which he has been served, or of which notice has not been given in the body of the indictment. In the trial at Newcastle, Black was not charged with the assault and abduction of Mandy Wilson in Stow, and, accordingly, under Scottish procedure evidence of that offence would not, in the circumstances of the present case, have been admissible. I say in the circumstances of the present case, because it is sometimes permitted to lead evidence of collateral matters which are not specified in a particular charge, but in my view, the abduction and assault of Mandy Wilson would not have qualified as a collateral matter in the present case. A further objection to the leading of this evidence under Scottish procedure would have been that it is not permitted to lead evidence of an accused's previous convictions at his trial for other offences. I believe the rule to be the same under English procedure but there, it is subject to the exception which was applied in Black's case. That exception does not in my view apply in Scotland.

Accordingly, if Black had been tried under Scottish procedure, the evidence relating to the abduction and assault on Mandy Wilson would not have been heard by the jury, and what seemed to me to be the mainstay of the prosecution case would therefore, not have surfaced. The remaining circumstantial evidence insofar as I can assess it from this book might not have been enough having regard to the defence evidence to persuade the jury beyond reasonable doubt of Black's guilt. In that situation the outcome might well have been an acquittal in the form of the Not Proven verdict either unanimously or by a majority, which in the Scottish system, where there are fifteen jurors, could have been by eight votes to seven. I should emphasise that this is pure speculation on my part, and reflects a personal point of view.

A Not Proven verdict, while it is an acquittal, is said to leave a stain on the character of an accused because the jury have not been prepared to go as far as saying that the accused is not guilty. Sad to say, in this day and age a Not Proven verdict does not seem to attract the same opprobrium as it used to, and most accused are well satisfied with such a verdict, because they know that they can never be tried again for the same offence.

Much discussion has taken place about the rights and wrongs of the Not Proven verdict. This is not the time or place to further that discussion. It is enough for me in commending this book to the reader simply to comment on this aspect of this intriguing case and to leave it to him to form his own opinion of what might have occurred in a different jurisdiction.

Mr Church has given us a splendid book in the 'Famous Trials' tradition, and there is virtue in the fact that it also raises questions of general importance. I wish it the success which it deserves.

The Honourable Lord Cowie,
Senator of the College of Justice (retired)
January 1996

INTRODUCTION

On Thursday, 19 May 1994 at Newcastle Crown Court, Robert Black, a forty-seven-year-old Scottish-born van driver who at the time of his arrest had been living in London, was given ten life sentences. Three of them were for murder and led the judge, Mr Justice Macpherson, to recommend that Black, whom he described as an 'extremely dangerous man', should serve not less than thirty-five years.

The trial of Robert Black was the culmination of a twelve-year police investigation. In the summer of 1982 Susan Claire Maxwell, an eleven-year-old schoolgirl, was abducted near her home at the Borders village of Cornhill in Northumbria. Thirteen days later her body was found half buried in a copse over 200 miles away near Uttoxeter in Staffordshire.

During the next six years two other young girls were abducted and killed, and an attempt was made to snatch a third, all in similar circumstances to those of the Susan Maxwell kidnapping. Then in 1990 a six-year-old girl was taken from the middle of the Lothian and Borders village of Stow. By a stroke of good fortune the abduction was witnessed; soon afterwards Robert Black was stopped while driving his van in the back of which his latest victim was found bound and gagged but still alive. For this crime he was later sentenced to life imprisonment.

Between Black's appearance at the High Court in Edinburgh and that at Newcastle Crown Court four years later, detectives from Lothian and Borders, Northumbria, West Yorkshire, Staffordshire, Nottinghamshire and Leicestershire amassed a vast quantity of circumstantial evidence that linked him irrefutably to the abductions and murders. This combined effort was arguably the most painstaking, thorough and well co-ordinated murder inquiry ever undertaken.

Murder: the ultimate crime. The taking of a fellow human being's life has always given rise to a gamut of emotions among those not even remotely involved. Fascination, horror and anguish are still experienced by most people when they read or hear about what has become a depressingly familiar crime. Gangland killings, often drug-related or induced; the slaying by partners and lovers, both hetero- and homosexual; the savagery inflicted by the young upon the old: these and other homicidal combinations assail our hardening sensibilities on an almost daily basis.

One kind of homicide in particular, that of children, is invariably greeted with universal opprobrium and distress. Opprobrium directed towards the perpetrator and distress felt not only for the young victim, but also for the distraught parents; besides being totally overwhelmed by their grief, they often harbour feelings of guilt and self-recrimination in their belief that they have failed to protect their offspring.

Many such cases have faded into obscurity. Others have remained in the public's consciousness. The Moors murders were committed over thirty years ago, but the names of Ian Brady and Myra Hindley are synonymous with child murder and still feature regularly in the news. People, many of whom were not born when the events spoken of took place, know of the merciless nature of the crimes which each was found guilty of committing.

Less well remembered are the crimes of Peter Griffiths, John Straffen, Arthur Albert Jones and Raymond Leslie Morris. Griffiths, a twenty-two-year-old ex-guardsman, was hanged in Walton Prison, Liverpool, in November 1948 for abducting and killing four-year-old June Devaney whom he had taken from her Blackburn hospital bed. John Straffen was a feeble-minded young man who, only six months after his release from an institute for the feeble-minded, strangled two small girls. Found to be insane at his trial at Taunton Assizes in October 1951, Straffen was committed to Broadmoor. From there he escaped after six months to be recaptured within a few hours, but not before he had strangled another little girl. Despite his insanity he was sentenced to death at his subsequent trial. Later reprieved, he is likely to remain in prison for the rest of his life. Straffen was nine years into his life sentence when Arthur Albert Jones, forty-four, strangled twelve-year-old Brenda Nash in October 1960, afterwards dumping her body on Yately Common near Camberley. In March of the following year Jones was sentenced to fourteen years' imprisonment for raping another young girl the previous September, a month before the murder of Brenda Nash. In prison Jones indiscreetly admitted to a fellow inmate that he was responsible for that murder. Word reached the authorities and, together with newly acquired evidence of identification, resulted in Jones being put on trial again, this time for murder. Found guilty, he was given a life sentence. Finally, there was Raymond Leslie Morris, a twenty-nine-year-old man who abducted, sexually assaulted and then killed Christine Ann Darby, seven years old, whose body was later found on desolate Cannock Chase.

These cases all attracted immense public interest at the time. A feature common to all four was that each of the victims was a female aged twelve years or under. Over twenty years later the pattern had not changed; Robert Black's victims were each in the same category. The outstanding difference between the early cases and that of Robert Black is the interval between the commission of the offence and the trial of the accused. The time gap in the case of Morris was eighteen months, in that of Griffiths, Straffen and Jones much less. On the other hand, the first known killing attributed to Robert Black, that of Susan Claire Maxwell in July 1982, occurred twelve years before he was brought to trial, while with the most recent, Sarah Harper, there was still an eight-year gap before his appearance at Newcastle Crown Court.

In this book I have endeavoured from the available facts to reconstruct the circumstances surrounding each abduction and murder, and to look at the factors in Black's early life that may have influenced and provided motivation for his later behaviour. Many of those who had known Robert Black in the years before he was returned to prison in 1994 variously described him as an 'oddball' or 'loner'; a workmate who kept to himself and a man who avoided adult female company.

A former inmate who was in Peterhead Prison when Black started a life sentence for abducting a little girl at the Scottish Borders village of Stow in July 1990, told me:

> He tried to be one of the lads, playing darts and sometimes football, but no one liked him. He seemed somehow proud of what he had done, or maybe he was just pleased at the thought that he had got the better of the police and got away with the three killings. He tried to talk to me alone sometimes, but I just couldn't handle him.

In the following pages I have aimed to convey something of the fatal psyche that encompassed Robert Black and which led ultimately to the violent and horrifying deaths of three little girls. Much of the story is also taken up with the lengthy and painstaking police investigation undertaken over twelve years to bring Black to justice. Criticism from various sources has been levelled at the police over their strategy, and some have said that it was only by a remarkable stroke of good fortune that Black was eventually captured. This may in part have been true; every detective hopes for a lucky break that will reward them for the hundreds of hours normally devoted to a murder inquiry. If this comes about it does not in any way detract from the effort that has gone before in tracking down the killer.

In the case of Robert Black his apprehension was only one step (albeit a crucial one) towards his eventual appearance in the Crown Court at Newcastle charged among other things with the abduction and murder of Susan Maxwell, Caroline Hogg and Sarah Harper. For almost four years following his arrest an unprecedented police effort had been devoted to gathering enough evidence to secure a conviction. As was his right, Robert Black had refused to co-operate with the detectives. It had been a task requiring dedication, perseverence and infinite attention to detail. As the weeks and months passed enough information was pains-takingly extracted from hundreds of documents to convince the Crown Prosecution Service that there was sufficient circumstantial evidence to justify proceeding against Robert Black with a fair chance of securing a conviction.

And so it proved; although the burden of proof is greater when the evidence is purely circumstantial, Robert Black was convicted on all counts. As he went to leave the dock after being sentenced, he turned to the detectives standing not an arm's length away. 'Well done, boys,' he said. Those three words uttered by the man they had sought for so long were probably the most satisfying accolade they would ever receive.

CHAPTER 1

EARLY DAYS

The ancient market town of Falkirk lies in the industrial region just over 20 miles west of Edinburgh. For long a centre of iron founding, aluminium rolling and other industries, in recent years this industrial core has been successfully integrated into burgeoning tourist and cultural projects.

It was at Falkirk's Royal Infirmary on Monday, 21 April 1947 that Robert Black gave his first awakening yell. His mother, twenty-four-year-old Jessie Hunter Black, was a factory worker who lived in the Dock House within the precincts of nearby Grangemouth docks. The daughter of a railway furnacemen, Jessie gave birth to her son illegitimately, at a time when such an event was almost universally frowned upon. The baby's father was never identified.

Robert Black grew up without ever knowing his mother. She started adoption proceedings a few weeks after he was born, but these were never formally completed. Instead when he was six months old he went to live with Mrs Isabel 'Betty' Tulip, an experienced foster mother who lived in the Argyllshire village of Kinlochleven. Situated at the head of Loch Leven, the village is only a few miles from Glencoe, site of the infamous massacre. It was here amid the Grampian mountains that young Robbie Black was to spend the next thirteen years.

Contemporary records indicate that he displayed anti-social tendencies from an early age. He caused problems before he started going to school, displaying aggressiveness and temper tantrums, particularly towards other children. Betty Tulip, with many years' experience of handling fractious children, found that young Robbie's behaviour was at times almost too much for even her to be able to contain.

His conduct did not improve when he started to attend the village primary school. Although Mrs Tulip ensured that he was always clean and tidily dressed, his outward appearance belied his proneness to bully other children, especially those younger and smaller than himself. As a former pupil at the school recalled many years later: 'Robbie always wanted to boss the other kids around, and if he didn't get his own way he used his fists. Sometimes he could get really vicious for such a wee lad.'

Furthermore, despite his foster mother's efforts to keep him clean, and to encourage him to take regular baths, the boy exuded an unpleasant body odour, an affliction that was to dog him into adulthood. Inevitably to local children he became known as 'Smelly Robbie Tulip'.

At home Robert Black continued his anti-social behaviour. Perhaps it was a sense of isolation, a feeling that he was somehow 'different' from other children that provoked his wilfulness. After she had abandoned him he had had no further contact with his natural mother who within a year had married Francis Hall, a Falkirk factory worker, by whom she had four children before they eventually emigrated to Australia.

Whatever the reason for his recalcitrant behaviour, Black survived his formative years without having a serious clash with authority. During that time, however, he had been tentatively experimenting with self-defilement and abuse by inserting small objects into his rectum. This was to be the prelude to the development of an unhealthy lifelong interest in young girls.

When he was eleven years old any feeling of security he may have felt while under Betty Tulip's wing was snatched away when she died. Her death was a devastating blow: Mrs Tulip was the nearest he had ever known to a mother. Furthermore she had tried to understand him, and had succeeded in exercising a modicum of control over him. It meant that he had to be found another home, a move that was to precipitate an ominous deterioration in his behaviour.

The welfare services found Robert Black a home with another family in Kinlochleven. It seems that while at his new home sexual awareness and deviancy began to feature increasingly in his young life. His foster mother was horrified to find out that he had been indecently interfering with a little girl in a public lavatory. She immediately reported the incident to the social workers with an urgent request that they find other accommodation for the boy.

Before arrangements were completed for Black to be moved away from Kinlochleven, another schoolgirl complained to the local policeman that Robbie Black had molested her at school. At a time when policemen still had discretion in such matters, the constable decided to deal with it summarily, rather than take him before a juvenile bench. He was probably aware in any case that young Black and his unsavoury behaviour would soon be leaving the village.

Shortly afterwards Robert Black left Kinlochleven, the village that had been his home for as long as he could remember. He moved to a mixed-sex children's home called Redding which was housed in a former Edwardian mansion outside Falkirk, the town where he was born.

The move was not a success; before long Black had reverted to his former aberrant behaviour. To the concern of Christine McCrae and her staff at the home, he availed himself of the opportunity afforded by joint games and activities to expose himself to the girls, and what was at times even more disturbing, to make undisguised sexual overtures and contact with them. Matters culminated when he forcibly removed the pants from a girl before staff were able to intervene. Following this episode it was decided that a mixed environment was inappropriate for such a sexually aware boy who seemed already to be rapidly becoming obsessed with young members of the opposite sex.

A case conference was convened at which staff members of Redding and representatives from welfare agencies met to consider the situation. It was decided that an establishment for boys only, where care, education and discipline were equally dispensed, would be the most suitable place for their recalcitrant young resident as he approached adolescence. Thus it came about that Robert Black found himself again on the move, this time to the Red House Care Home at Musselburgh, a small burgh on the Firth of Forth adjacent to Portobello. With only forty resident boys, it was considered that supervision and control were likely to be more effective than at Redding.

However, evil was lurking within the walls of the Red House. Within weeks of his arrival a member of staff commenced a systematic programme of abuse against Robert Black. This continued for three years and did not come to light until many years later, long after the perpetrator was dead. It has been suggested that this experience at the Red House may have led directly to Black's later degeneracy. However, it must be remembered that his sexual compulsions had commenced before he went to the Red House. His experience there may well have exacerbated the situation, but his interest in matters sexual needed little encouragement.

The proximity of the Musselburgh home to Portobello – the latter was only a walk or a short bus ride away – meant that during his stay at the home Robert Black was to become familiar with the resort and the surrounding district, knowledge that may well have been useful to him later. Part of Portobello's appeal for the boy lay in the two swimming pools it boasted in the 1960s.

For five years Robert Black, or Boy Number 28 as he was listed, lived at the Red House. Academically he was above average, gaining a place at Musselburgh Grammar School, while his interest in sport was undiminished. Among other sporting activities he played as goalkeeper for the Red House soccer team, and gained a lifesaving badge at swimming. Despite this he remained a loner and had few friends. It is likely that distancing himself from his peers was symptomatic of the abuse to which he was being subjected. He shared an attic dormitory with several other boys, but it is not known if any of his companions were victims of the abuser. If so, the perpetrator succeeded for many years in keeping knowledge of his depravity from the eyes and ears of the authorities.

When he reached the age of sixteen Robert Black left school; simultaneously his tenure at the Red House came to an end. By then his own sexuality increasingly preoccupied him, a shortcoming that his experiences at the home had encouraged.

Still under the wing of the child welfare agencies, Black moved across Scotland to Greenock, the shipbuilding and industrial town 20 miles west of Glasgow. Here he was found lodgings in another boys' home, and obtained his first job as a butcher's delivery boy. Years later he admitted that during this employment he took every opportunity to molest little girls, an activity that was to culminate in his first court appearance. It was for an offence which was the precursor of a pattern of criminal behaviour that was to remain his trademark.

It took place on a summer's evening in 1963 when Black was in a local park watching a group of schoolgirls playing on the swings. He watched them as they drifted away until only one small girl remained. By now the growing urge he had been feeling had become irresistible. It was an impulse that was an innate component of Robert Black's genetic make-up. At times it would be repressed – he would occasionally experience feelings of disgust or remorse – but more usually a wave of sexual frenzy would overwhelm him with dire consequences for the young female who had triggered off his lust.

Black approached the girl and chatted to her for a few minutes before inviting her into a derelict air raid shelter on the pretext that some kittens had made it their home. As soon as his unsuspecting victim had entered the dimly lit building, Black held her tightly by the throat until she was unconscious before indecently assaulting her. He then ran away leaving the girl to regain consciousness alone and terrified. Soon afterwards she was found wandering nearby crying hysterically.

Robert Black was arrested the next day and subsequently appeared at Greenock Sheriff court charged with lewd and libidinous behaviour. After reference had been made to a psychiatrist's report suggesting that the offence had been an isolated incident, and that he was not in need of treatment, Black was admonished, a sentencing option available only to Scottish courts and amounting to nothing more than a warning as to his future behaviour.

The social services viewed the incident rather more seriously than the court and decided that Robert Black should leave Greenock and return to a district with which he was already familiar, Grangemouth near Falkirk. Here he was found lodgings with an elderly couple, the first occasion in which he had lived anywhere other than in a children's home since leaving Kinlochleven. The change of abode did nothing to discourage his sexual proclivity; he was still in the habit of touching and fondling young girls whenever the opportunity presented itself.

Despite his penchant for very young females, it was during Black's time at Grangemouth that he met his only known adult girfriend. He met Pamela Hodgson at a youth club in the town and was immediately attracted to her. They went out together for several months until Pamela could no longer tolerate his deviant sexual demands or his offensive body odour, and wrote to him ending their relationship. Black later insisted that he had been devastated by the break-up. He had apparently been hoping that he and Pamela would become engaged, and for a long time he had refused to accept the fact that she had left him.

Soon after Black and Pamela Hodgson had parted company the couple with whom he lodged found out that he had reverted to his former habits. They were appalled to learn that when their young granddaughter had been visiting them Black had regularly been indecently interfering with her. Their initial instinct had been to notify the police, but on reflection they rejected that idea through fear of the trauma to which their grand-daughter might later be subjected. Instead they told their young lodger to leave the house immediately.

No doubt thankful for this let-off, Black carried on with his daily routine. He was working for a builders' supply company and one day soon after he had been thrown out of his lodgings he was called into the office. There he was surprised and angry to be told that his services were no longer required.

Humiliated by this peremptory dismissal, Black decided to leave Grangemouth and return to Kinlochleven, the place that he had always looked back on as home. There he found work as a driver and lodgings with a couple living in Appin Street. Before long his reputation had caught up with him; together with his already questionable behaviour, this brought him to the notice of many people in the Highland community and on several occasions he was remonstrated with by police and the local folk.

It seemed inevitable that sooner or later Robert Black would come into serious conflict with the law. It came about within a year of his arrival in Kinlochleven with the commission of a serious assault on the six-year-old daughter of the couple with whom he was staying, and for whom he was baby-sitting. This time he was not as fortunate as he had been at Grangemouth as the child's parents lost no time in reporting the matter to the police. His luck deserted him further when, after pleading guilty to three cases of indecent assault, he was sentenced in March 1963 to Borstal training. This he was to complete at Polmont Borstal at Brightons, near his former home at Redding, Falkirk. Not yet twenty, Robert Black was now a confirmed paedophile.

Following his release from Polmont after twelve months, Black decided that his future lay elsewhere than in Scotland. After considering the options he decided to follow the path trodden by many thousands of his compatriots and to go and live among the Sassanachs in London.

CHAPTER 2

LONDON

To a migrant from the north, London can present a daunting as well as an exciting image. Its sheer size and area, together with its bewildering geographic layout, of which the newcomer will have had a foretaste as his train nears King's Cross through the capital's northern approaches, have caused many a new arrival to question his decision to seek a new life south of the border.

Although when he arrived Black soon found a bed-sitter in one of the dingy streets around King's Cross station, it was not until much later that he obtained regular work. In the meantime he contented himself with casual employment. One job, that of a life-guard at Hornsey swimming baths, did not last long; he was sacked for allegedly indecently assaulting a girl swimmer! He moved several times, but never strayed far from the area around King's Cross. He spent most of his free time in the local public house where he soon became recognised as an above average darts player.

Tony Bailey, one of Robert Black's drinking companions at that time, remembered him as 'a big fellow who could throw a good arrow. Compared with some of the others he didn't drink a lot, lager and shandies I believe. He seemed more taken up with the game, and after he had finished playing he used to go home before closing time.'

It was in 1972 that Black met the couple who were to provide him with a home for almost twenty years. He was playing darts in the Three Crowns at Stoke Newington when he got into conversation with Eddie and Kathy Rayson. Eddie and Kathy were fellow Scots from Musselburgh, the town that Black knew well but which for him held only unhappy memories. During the course of the evening Black brought up the subject of lodgings, telling his new friends that he was unhappy with his current accommodation and asking Eddie if he had a spare room that he could rent him. Eddie Rayson thought about the matter, and after discussing it briefly with his wife invited Black with some reluctance to move into a spare attic room in their house at Stamford Hill.

Kathy Rayson was more amenable to the idea of Black moving in with them. The Raysons already had four children living at home in their four-storeyed Victorian villa, and Kathy considered that having an extra person living there, particularly one who would be contributing to the family income, would make little difference. Thus it came about that in the autumn of 1970, Robert Black moved in with the people who, despite Eddie's reservations, were soon to accept him as one of the family.

John Banks, another pal from the days when Black had first arrived in London, recalled how he changed after he had moved in with the Raysons: 'He seemed to be more settled, and certainly more sociable. Before Robbie moved he never had a lot to say. Afterwards he was much more chatty, talking about his job and other things.'

It is highly unlikely that the 'other things' included the growing collection of pornographic books, pictures and videos Black was accumulating in his room. Knowledge of these did not emerge until much later, although several years after Black had moved into 31 West Bank, Raymond Rayson, with adolescent curiosity, had entered his room during his absence. What he discovered shocked him; inside an unlocked suitcase had been a selection of pornographic photographs, mainly of children. Stunned at what he had found, Raymond left the room and kept the incident to himself until he testified at Robert Black's trial.

Black was also a keen photographer and over the years he assembled an impressive array of photographic and video equipment. Not for him though holiday snaps or conventional camera studies. When the contents of his room were eventually revealed, they were found to include several dozen self-portraits of him posing in obscene attitudes, many with various implements and everyday household items inserted into his anus. Another of his interests was body-building, and Black prided himself on his physique.

Careful to conceal his deviance from those who knew him (although Kathy Rayson later suspected her lodger of enjoying pornographic videos), Robert Black was keen to portray himself as a 'good bloke', content to live quietly with the Raysons and to earn enough money to enable him to enjoy his pool and darts at the local pub. It was his apparent normality that concealed his menace.

Several of those people that had got to know Black well during his years in London were confounded when in 1990 he was arrested for child abduction in the Border village of Stow. Four years later their incredulity was stretched further when their former workmate, drinking companion and member of the pub darts team was convicted at Newcastle of three child abductions and murders.

John Banks again: 'I had known Robbie Black for close on twenty years, and although at times he seemed a bit of an oddball – he never eyed women up like some of us did, in fact he was more likely to annoy them with some of his remarks – it never struck me that he was capable of those sorts of things. It was unbelievable.'

To the Raysons Black had been a trouble-free lodger. Kathy in particular had felt sorry for her lonely fellow countryman, and in many ways had pampered him. Black had responded by buying her an occasional bunch of flowers or box of chocolates, and ensuring that he never overlooked family birthdays or Christmas time.

The Rayson menfolk were more wary of him; admittedly he had never defaulted with his rent and often he accompanied them to the pub. Nevertheless they had occasionally had misgivings about him, none of them warranting anything more than discussion among themselves. At 31 West Bank, Black ate his meals with the family, but otherwise kept to himself. Locked away in his attic room, from which could frequently be heard the sound of his favourite country and western music coming from his expensive stereo equipment, he spent time watching pornographic videos and engaging in other bizarre activity.

The body odour had never left Black, and to the Rayson children he became known as 'Smelly Bob', a soubriquet that he seemed to accept without resentment. To those who knew him during the '60s and '70s it appeared that his consuming interest was darts. He had a passing interest in football which extended at one time to his being given a trial by a well-known non-league club, but playing darts and mixing with the dart-playing fraternity seemed to be his main recreation. That he was a very good player there is little doubt. He played regularly for the Baring Arms pub team which competed in the North London Super Darts League. It was while on the dart-playing circuit that he played against Eric Bristow who went on to become five times world champion.

At about this time in the early '70s Black obtained part-time employment as a barman in a Stoke Newington public house. He was a good worker who was trusted by the landlord and his wife to the extent that they would leave him to look after their children when they went out together. Occasionally Black also took the children swimming at the local pool. At no time did their parents feel cause for concern when he was with the children, and it was never suggested that he behaved improperly towards them. Maybe Black had no wish to tarnish his local reputation by doing anything which, had it led to exposure, would have created serious trouble for him.

It is futile to speculate on the extent of Robert Black's deviant activity while he was living in London. Almost certainly he continued stalking and molesting young girls during his travels around the country. Some of these incidents may have been reported, others not. If, however, Black appeared in court during this time he was dealt with leniently as no record could be found of his having been to prison. Sacked from his job as a life-guard because of his indecent behaviour soon after he had arrived in London, at home Black confined himself to viewing porno-graphic videos and reading porno magazines; together with acts of self-debasement, this seemed temporarily to satisfy his libido.

By the mid-1970s, although he was still working on a casual basis, Black was driving fairly regularly for a living. He had bought a white Fiat van which he used both for work and as a runabout. In 1976 he started working for a company with whom he was to remain until he was arrested fourteen years later. Poster Dispatch and Storage was a firm whose fleet of vans delivered posters to several dozen locations around Britain. For Robert Black the job was particularly inviting; it enabled him, at the company's expense and with the minimum of supervision, to travel the length and breadth of the land. Initially from his East London base in Hoxton, his favourite run was to the south coast which with its many resorts and beaches provided him with ample opportunity to watch children in swimsuits playing on the sand.

Like the other drivers, however, he was expected to make wide-ranging deliveries to other parts of the country. A route with which he became familiar was that which took him to the Midlands. In August 1981 John and Angie Rayson moved into a house at Donisthorpe, a village in Leicestershire not far from Ashby-de-la-Zouch. From then onwards he often called in to see the couple when passing through the district. Angie Rayson always felt uneasy in Black's presence, although she was unable to pin-point the reason for her disquiet.

It was not long before Black familiarised himself with a number of alternative routes to various destinations, an attribute of which he often spoke, although his fellow drivers were less enthused; as one of them pointed out at his trial: 'Robbie would come in and say he had found a different way to do this and that. Half the time nobody took any notice, because they always seemed to be longer than the ones we used.'

Black's fellow workers at PDS had ambivalent feelings about him. Thomas Cusack trained him when he first joined the company. They had become friendly and Black had visited his home on several occasions. Robert Black's former boss, Raymond Baker, also considered him to be a friend prior to his arrest in 1990. However, Eric Mould, the general manager of PDS, later said, 'He had a personal freshness problem. He smelled.'

This unpleasant affliction remained with Black throughout, although generally the PDS employees tended to disregard it. A matter about which he was more self-conscious was his retreating hairline. When Black had first worked for PDS he had not yet lost most of his hair and tried to disguise its loss by flicking the remaining strands across his head in what his workmates amusingly referred to as his 'Bobby Charlton' style.

Little is ever likely to be known about Robert Black's movements between joining PDS, in 1976, and July 1982. Extensive inquiries by detectives investigating other abductions and murders, notably those of two thirteen-year-olds, April Fabb in 1969 and Genette Tate in August 1978, have so far failed to connect him with these, or the mystery surrounding the disappearance of other young girls during that period. The inquiries are still being actively pursued in the hope that eventually they will either incriminate or absolve him from involvement.

These inquiries have extended to mainland Europe as police are aware that Black was in the habit of travelling to the Continent periodically to stock up on pornographic videos and magazines. On another occasion he drove to Tourtoirac in the Dordogne to view a house that Eddie and Kathy Rayson had bought with the aim of settling abroad.

It seems that Black's depravity was building up to its climax during the years leading up to 1982. Several people had occasionally been given lifts in his van and recall the stench inside the vehicle. 'He gave me a lift home from work once, and that was enough. The smell in the van was awful,' recalled Mark Stonehouse, while George Brown wondered at the time why the van stank. 'I remember thinking, "He's only carrying posters, I wonder where the smell is coming from?" Later of course I found out.' The presence of a rolled-up mattress in the back of the van also caused speculation. 'I wondered why Robbie carried a mattress in the back. Most drivers used a sleeping bag if they slept in their van overnight,' commented Ian Barclay. Black had told the other drivers that he had the mattress to sleep on during overnight journeys, but when other assorted items were later found in the van, the mattress assumed a more sinister significance.

Years later Robert Black admitted that during his cross-country trips he was in the habit of pulling into a lay-by, getting into the back of the van, undressing and then squeezing into little girls' underclothing and swimsuits, before abusing himself. He would also interrupt his delivery runs to carry out other acts of self-abuse, often entailing the insertion into his anus of one or more of a variety of objects he took with him for this purpose.

When not at work Black resumed his usual routine. By the early 1980s life at 31 West Bank had changed little, apart from most of the children having grown up. The two eldest boys, John and Raymond, would often accompany Black for a drink and a game of darts or pool. Black would invariably dress in a T-shirt, track suit bottoms and trainers on these occasions. Together with his offensive body odour, it is not surprising that women found him unappealing. Kathy Rayson encouraged him to take regular baths, but for the most part her urgings seem to have been unsuccessful. In turn, Black showed very little interest in young adult females.

As time passed, the attitude of his workmates tended to be one of toleration rather than of active like or dislike. He was always prepared to have a game of snooker, but only rarely did he go out for a drink with the other drivers. He had visited one or two of them at their homes and they in turn had been to his lodgings, but only after he had hidden away evidence of his secret obsessions.

At the Hoxton base of PDS, Black pleased some of his colleagues while others were aggrieved by his willingness to undertake weekend deliveries to Scotland. Such trips were unpopular with the married men, and to them his offer was welcome. However, their appreciation was tempered when they learnt that he was prepared to go on these extended journeys at weekday rates of pay, rather than at the enhanced weekend rates. Black had good reason for this apparent beneficence; such journeys provided him with the opportunities he sought, such as the one that arose in July 1982.

CHAPTER 3

THE KILLING YEARS

30 July–1 August 1982

The events of Friday, 30 July 1982 near Coldstream had their origins the previous day over 300 miles away in East London. When Derek Wilcox, a PDS driver, arrived for work that day he discovered that over the coming weekend he was scheduled to make a delivery trip to Scotland. Wilcox was faced with a dilemma; there was a crisis at home concerning his son that demanded his presence. He explained the situation to his employer and asked to be rescheduled. He found that his domestic problems aroused little sympathy, and a heated exchange took place which culminated in Wilcox being summarily dismissed.

The company then had to find a driver who was prepared at short notice to make the Scottish run. Presagefully Robert Black then arrived for work and agreed immediately to take the place of Wilcox the next day.

The following morning Black set out on his journey north. As he threaded his Fiat van across London, he was filled with a sense of well-being. It promised to be another fine hot day; he would earn himself a sizeable bonus and he had several poster deliveries to make across southern and central Scotland; who knew what the day would bring forth . . . ?

He crossed the North Circular Road and joined the A1, a road he knew well. After leaving the northern suburbs of London Black headed towards Hatfield. His long drive north passed off uneventfully; it is likely that he stopped once or twice, maybe at a lay-by or transport café. His first verifiable halt was sometime after 1 p.m. when he pulled into a filling station at Stannington, a few miles south of Morpeth, to refuel with diesel. Little was he aware as he handed over in payment the fuel credit card supplied by PDS that the transaction was to be resurrected twelve years later.

After Morpeth, Black turned off the A1 on to the A697. This was one of his favourite routes into Scotland. Passing through the rolling Northumbrian countryside with the Cheviot Hills to the west, it carried much less traffic than the A1, and throughout its 65-mile length until it joined the A68, it afforded a more relaxing and picturesque alternative.

As Robert Black drove along the A697, maybe pausing for a time at one of his favourite cafés, ahead of him in the Border town of Coldstream, a pretty eleven-year-old schoolgirl wearing a yellow T-shirt and shorts was happily playing tennis with a young girlfriend.

Just before 4 p.m. on Friday, 30 July 1982, Robert Black drove round the right-hand bend on the English side of the border with Scotland and approached the stone bridge spanning the River Tweed. Across the bridge he negotiated a sharp bend to the left and headed towards Coldstream town centre. Then he spotted her; walking along the pavement in the direction from which he had come, Susan Claire Maxwell, swinging her tennis racket as she made her way home to Cramond Hill farm. The urge . . .

Black only glimpsed her as he passed, but it was enough for him to decide. A few yards further on he turned his van round and retraced his route. He overtook her as she approached the bridge; on the other side he looked for a suitable place in which to wait. A hundred yards further on was an entrance set back from the road leading into a field. It was wide enough for him to reverse his van and was not immediately apparent to anyone approaching by car or on foot. Robert Black watched and waited. He watched as the girl drew nearer; she was on his side of the road and after crossing the bridge would reach him in less than a minute. She came nearer . . . nearer . . . *now* . . .

Robert Black's first delivery on this trip was at Edinburgh, the next a few miles away at Dunfermline. As he drove on along the A697 that afternoon, it is not known whether Susan Maxwell was still alive. Although she was already bound and gagged in the back of the van, there was a possibility that her nightmare was not over and that she survived until the next day. Whether alive or dead, Susan Maxwell was in the back of Black's van while he made his Scottish deliveries. After calling first at Edinburgh, he drove across the Forth Bridge with its view of Rosyth Dockyard and the Firth of Forth wending its way towards the North Sea, to the Royal Burgh of Dunfermline, former residence of Scottish kings and the Scottish capital 1000 years previously.

From Dunfermline Black had a choice of routes to Dundee. By this time it was late afternoon and this probably dissuaded him from taking either the long coastal road via St Andrews or the meandering route through Glenrothes. Instead, despite his preference for main and secondary roads, he is likely to have taken the M60 motorway as far as Kinross before turning off north-eastwards on the A91, flanked by Pitmedden Forest and the Lomond hills.

After delivering at Dundee Black was faced with an arduous journey across Scotland to Glasgow. He did not deliver there until around midnight. The time factor was to be of crucial importance later.

With his final delivery made, there remained for Robert Black only the journey south back to London. On the way south he had to dispose of the body lying behind him. After leaving Glasgow Black looked for a suitable place to pull in for the night. Eventually he found one where he clambered into the back of his van and settled himself down until morning.

The next day Robert Black set out on the final lap of his journey. Driving down the A74, he stopped at Carlisle to refuel before continuing on to the M6. The road from Glasgow to East London was one with which he was familiar; he enjoyed seeking out alternative routes to the ones more generally used, preferring therefore to cut across on the A50 to the M1 rather than keeping to the M6 motorway, thus avoiding the hold-ups and congestion around the Spaghetti Junction interchange. A further advantage of this route was that he could divert for a few miles and visit John Rayson and his family in Donisthorpe.

On this Saturday in July 1982, Black had a more urgent matter to resolve: to rid himself of Susan Maxwell's body. As he left behind the pottery towns of Kidsgrove and Stoke-on-Trent, and continued into the undulating North Staffordshire countryside, he considered what to do. He knew that he dare not delay a decision for much longer as once back on a motorway and heading towards London, there was a much-increased risk of being seen. As he approached Uttoxeter he had an idea; turning right towards Stafford at the junction with the A518, he drove through Uttoxeter and regained the open country beyond. Soon he saw a sign indicating a parking place ahead. A short distance further on he pulled into a lay-by and was pleased to see that a small wood lay a few yards back from the road.

By this time it was getting dark; traffic was light and after a quick look around he was satisfied that no one appeared to be about. It took him only a few seconds to lift Susan Maxwell's body from the van and carry her into the wood. Once he had gained the shadow of the trees he found a small hollow; placing the body on the ground, he covered it roughly with undergrowth and stepped back, satisfied that his victim would remain for the time being undiscovered.

Mystery surrounds Robert Black's movements from the late evening of Saturday, 31 July, when he stopped at the Loxley lay-by, to his refuelling stop at the Watford Gap at 11 p.m. Sunday evening. Nothing emerged during the police investigation to indicate that he had stopped at John Rayson's house, so it can only be assumed that he spent another night in his van. From the Watford Gap it did not take Black long to complete his journey. Soon after Sunday midnight he pulled up outside 31 West Bank, Stamford Hill, his Scottish business completed.

August 1982–July 1983

Life slipped back into its normal routine for Robert Black after his foray into Scotland. Nino Barboretti was the proprietor of a King's Cross café who had known Black since soon after his arrival in London in 1968, Nino had a particular reason for recalling the summer of 1982 as he had put his establishment up for sale with the intention of returning with his family permanently to Italy. He remembered that Black 'was always affable, but was never a great talker. He would always try to sit at a table by himself, where he would sometimes read a paper, or more often just look out of the window. By then he had been working regularly for some time, so often we did not see him for days on end.'

After reading the news that Susan Maxwell's body had been discovered on 12 August, Black closely followed the progress of the police inquiry. He was aware of the possibility that someone had spotted him, either at the time he had snatched the girl, or when he had dumped her. As days and weeks extended into months, and, with diminishing media interest, the case gradually faded from the public's mind, he knew that the police would not have relaxed their efforts to find him; nevertheless, as time passed he felt increasingly confident that he would remain undetected.

Black was still playing darts regularly and if away and down for a match in London would make every effort to return home in time. He also continued to make occasional trips to the Continent to acquire pornographic videos and magazines to add to his collection. Although he was familiar with most sources in London where he could obtain such material, he knew many places in Europe where he could buy films and other items which particularly appealed to him, much of it unobtainable or prohibitively expensive at home.

As 1982 drew to a close, Robbie Black joined in the Rayson Christmas festivities and toasted in the New Year. Detectives suspect that this was a mere pause in his activity, and that during his journeyings to various parts of the country Black continued his wayward lifestyle, ranging from watching swimsuited children to actively molesting them. Many incidents were probably not reported due to the parents' reluctance to subject their children to the intimate questioning and court proceedings that might arise.

Such was the situation prevailing in the summer of 1983. On Wednesday, 6 July, with the promise of fine weather to come, Black found himself scheduled to make a run to Scotland and the north of England the next day. As was usually the case Black would do the weekend trip to enable other drivers to be at home on Saturday and Sunday.

July 1983

On Friday, 8 July 1983, the inquest into Susan Maxwell's death was reconvened at Uttoxeter. After hearing evidence from the Home Office pathologist, Dr Scholz van der Merwe, the East Staffordshire coroner Mr Edward Huntback recorded an open verdict.

Two days later Robert Black was looking forward to returning to Scotland. On this trip he had posters to drop off near Portobello at the depot of Mills and Allen. He knew the area well from the five years he had spent at Musselburgh, and although those had not been happy times he had learnt that at this time of the year Portobello would be full of holiday-makers and day trippers with their children.

Black set out on Thursday morning and took his usual route up the Great North Road. His first delivery was at Gateshead. He arrived on Tyneside in the early evening and made his drop before continuing for a few miles until he found a suitable spot at which to pull in for the night.

The next morning he kept to the A1 rather than diverting through Coldstream as he had a year before. A stop at Belford for diesel, and then on past Berwick-upon-Tweed towards Edinburgh. The scenic Northumbrian and Borders countryside was at its best, and occasionally the North Sea could be seen to the east, the sun reflecting off its shimmering surface.

By early on Friday afternoon Black was driving through Musselburgh along a road he had trod so many times before when living at the Red House. Just off the Portobello Road was the Mills and Allen depot where he made his delivery.

It was hot and sunny and the crowds were thronging the promenade. Fun City amusement park was full and the beach was crowded with young and old playing or lying in the sun, or venturing into the water. For Robert Black it was a scene he remembered and one that he savoured. He left his van in a car-park near the promenade and wandered along the sea front watching the activity and pausing every now and again to peer into some of the amusement arcades before sauntering into the amusement park.

He strolled a short distance inland and lounged for a while against the railings of a small park, rolling himself a cigarette while watching some children playing on the swings. After a few minutes he moved away as it was nearly time for him to start back on his return journey. Then he saw her: a pretty little thing, hair tied back in bunches and wearing a blue and white dress with pink trainers. He watched her as she walked towards the promenade; he hesitated for a few seconds and then the urge welled up inside him. It was an opportunity not to be missed.

As Caroline Hogg walked towards the sea front, oblivious of the man trailing her, she acknowledged some children whom she knew. She did not stop as she was in a hurry to get to where the people and the excitement were. One of the children Caroline passed was fourteen-year-old Jennifer Booth, now Mrs Nadle, who remembers seeing Caroline and then a short distance behind 'a fat, scruffy-looking man'. Mrs Nadle went on, 'They seemed to be on their own. I didn't take much notice, it was just that I had seen Caroline around, and the man somehow seemed out of place, not casual as you expect at the seaside, but really scruffy.'

Near the sea wall Caroline sat down; she felt tired and was already thinking of going home. After a few minutes she got up and started to wander back in the direction of Bridge Street. A short distance away a man was sitting on a bench. He spoke to her and seemed nice. 'Yes, please,' she would like a ride on the roundabout. 'No,' she hadn't been to Fun City. He smiled and held her hand as together they walked a few yards to the amusement park. To passers-by the scene was not unusual: a little girl out with her dad at the seaside. Holding his hand while laughing and chattering happily, Caroline clambered aboard the double-decker bus on the children's carousel while the man stood and watched her. This was fun; what a nice man. She alighted from the roundabout and grasped again the hand of her new friend. That's funny, I wonder why we are going into the car-park? In the distance Caroline thought she could hear her mother calling her name . . .

Robert Black's next destination was the Mills and Allen depot in Glasgow. He arrived there in just over an hour, made his delivery and was soon on his way south towards England. He crossed the border during the early hours of Saturday morning and soon afterwards stopped to refuel at Carlisle. Thereafter detectives were unable to retrace his precise route, or the timetable surrounding his disposal of Caroline Hogg's body. It is assumed that he followed his usual route down the M6 motorway, turning off as before on to the A50 before continuing on to the A444. What will never be known for certain is the time Caroline Hogg died. I believe it to have been most likely during Friday night sometime after her abductor had left Carlisle. She may have already died from suffocation before Black stopped to refuel, or she may have died at his hand later.

Another question: when was her body deposited in the ditch at the Twycross lay-by? Again one can only balance the probabilities. Black is known to have made another stop for diesel on Saturday morning at a filling station in Staffordshire, only a few miles from where she was eventually found. A month after Caroline's abduction a witness came forward and reported that on the morning of Saturday, 9 July at a lay-by situated a short distance away from the one in which she was discovered, he had seen a young girl making what he described as 'a dash for freedom' from a man resembling the photofit of Robert Black. Although at the time police regarded the alleged incident seriously, it was never confirmed and cannot be relied upon. Nevertheless Saturday morning is the time that Black was likely to have been in the vicinity of the Twycross lay-by.

The alternative to the body having been dumped on the Saturday is that Black kept it in the back of his van when he returned to London. Three days later he returned with a poster delivery to Bedworth in Warwickshire. It is possible that before or after making the delivery he travelled the few miles further along the A444 through Nuneaton to Twycross. This hypothesis was supported by an entomologist who during a later examination opined that the body's state of decomposition indicated that Tuesday, 12 July was the earliest date at which it could have been left at Twycross. Both theories are awful to contemplate, but surely the image of Robert Black going about his daily business with the corpse of Caroline Hogg in the back of his van defies belief.

July 1983–August 1986

Although between 1983 and 1986 Robert Black was apparently leading a normal, uneventful life, the reality was that he was still absorbed in his paedophiliac obsession. Secure behind the door of his room at 31 West Bank, he would spend hours reading and looking at pornographic magazines and pictures, or with his eyes riveted to the screen, watching erotic videos featuring children, 'Lollitots' as they were called, often to a background of his favourite country and western music, played to disarm other occupants in the house. At other times Black continued to patronise the Baring Arms where as a member of the darts team he partook of his other favourite pastime.

It was on his travels that he was able to bring to life his fantasies. It was during the 1980s that Robert Black was at the pinnacle of his evil doing. By the end of 1983 he is known to have abducted and slain two children. As he later admitted, he was always on the look-out for likely victims; some were fortunate enough to have escaped with their lives after having been subjected to whatever horror Black could devise for them in the back of his van. Others were perhaps not so fortunate, many detectives remaining convinced that he was responsible for other unsolved child murders from the late 1970s onwards.

The year 1986 did not start well for Robert Black. Although experienced, he was by no means a good driver and since joining PDS had been involved in several minor accidents. This had resulted in the company having to pay higher insurance premiums for their fleet of vehicles. Furthermore Black's time-keeping was poor. So early in the year, considered overall to be more of a liability than an asset, he was sacked.

However there was a reversal in his fortunes soon afterwards. Poster Dispatch and Storage was taken over by new owners who in turn were soon bought out by two former employees. They were aware of Black's willingness to undertake work that often entailed long journeys at short notice and at weekends and were prepared to re-employ him providing he bought and insured his own van. Black had no hesitation in accepting the deal.

It was another routine trip for Robert Black. As he set out from East London on the morning of Wednesday, 26 March 1986, he had a series of deliveries to make across the north of England from Hull to Brighouse. On his way north there were also a couple of drop-offs to be made in the Midlands, so it was past midday when he struck out from Leicester towards Hull.

The afternoon passed without incident. Hull, on to York and then south-westwards along the A64 to Leeds. The weather was not promising so Black decided to continue to Brighouse, make his deliveries and then return to Leeds for the day's last calls. His final delivery was to be at the premises of Myles and Spencer, on the southern outskirts of the town. Before arriving there, Black refuelled his van. The weather had worsened, low clouds scudding across the sky giving warning of heavy rain later, so he considered parking overnight in the builder's yard adjacent to Myles and Spencer, sleeping in the back of the van.

Not just yet though; he could feel the urge creeping over him, so as it was only quarter to six he would leave his van across the road from Myles and Spencer and have a stroll. You never knew who might be about . . .

Black spent the next hour alternately roaming and driving around the local streets. Just before half-past six a Mrs Appleyard took her dog out for its evening walk. A few minutes later as she was walking up Clough Street it started to rain, and she noticed a bearded man wearing glasses getting into the driver's seat of a white van which was parked almost opposite Brunswick Place. A few minutes later she saw that the van had gone.

Black saw Mrs Appleyard looking at him as she walked past, so he drove a hundred yards away and stopped at the end of Charles Street. Although by now it was raining hard, he left his vehicle to take a final look around. Moments later he saw a small figure emerge from the house at the far end of Brunswick Place. Huddled into an anorak, its hood up, and with only a thin pair of legs wearing white socks visible, she came up the cul-de-sac before cutting through a 'snicket'* into Page Street. Black followed her and caught up as she entered the corner shop. He followed her in but left before her and returned to wait in the shadows at the end of the cul-de-sac. Seconds later she reappeared from the 'snicket', carrying a loaf of bread and some bags of crisps.

Swiftly Black moved behind her and lifted her bodily, a hand clamped

* Snicket: North Country dialect meaning a passageway between walls.

over her mouth. While her spindly legs kicked out futilely, he carried the girl to his van parked a few yards away . . .

A post-mortem examination revealed that Sarah Harper had not died immediately. After being gagged, she had been subjected to a violent and sustained sexual attack which included rape, with or without the aid of an instrument, and had also suffered severe head injuries. There are two possible courses that Black could have adopted after he had snatched the child. (1) He may have immediately driven south to a spot near the village of Ratcliffe on Soar, a few miles south of Nottingham, and there violated her before dumping her unconscious body in the River Soar, a tributary of the Trent. After then spending the remainder of the night at or near Ratcliffe, he could have driven to Lincoln to make a delivery sometime the following morning, perhaps returning later to visit John Rayson at Donisthorpe before driving down the M1 to London. After refuelling at Newport Pagnell sometime after 7 p.m. he would have been home in Stamford Hill well before midnight. (2) He could have first driven across to Lincoln with his victim in the back of his van and made his delivery; from there returning to Ratcliffe and dumping her in the river. The attack on Sarah Harper could have been carried out sometime during this journey. From Ratcliffe a run down the motorway, stopping to refuel during the early hours of Thursday, 27 March, before continuing home.

A witness later came forward to say that he had seen a white van with a bare-headed man standing by the passenger door, parked in a gateway off the B6540 near Nottingham between 9.10 p.m. and 9.15 p.m. on Wednesday evening. This report was taken seriously by the police and gave credence to the first hypothesis.

Sarah Harper's murder is the last that has so far been attributed to Robert Black. Several other unresolved disappearances and killings of young girls occurred before and after Sarah's death about which detectives have continued to question him since his conviction.

Following his March 1986 Midlands foray, life for Black went on as before. He was aware that another massive hunt was on to find Sarah Harper's killer, but after his initial concern that he may have left one or more clues had faded, he relaxed, secure in the belief that he had succeeded again in avoiding detection by withdrawing into the anonymity of the distant metropolis. He asked himself how the police could possibly connect him with abductions and the disposal of bodies at locations as far afield and diverse as Scotland, northern England and the Midlands? How indeed?

Robert Black may not have felt so secure had he been aware of the police inquiries that had been pursued so relentlessly since the disappearance of Susan Maxwell in July 1982. During those four years the intensity of the investigation may have fluctuated, other demands inevitably requiring the allocation of police time and resources, but throughout that period there had remained a resolute core of detectives determined to capture a man who they were convinced posed a constant and terrible threat to young females across the country while he remained at liberty.

CHAPTER 4

WHERE IS SUSAN?

July–August 1982

For those travelling north from Newcastle along the overcrowded A1, a quieter and more scenic route is provided by the A697. Skirting Rothbury Forest and the Cheviot Hills, crossing the land that for centuries was bitterly fought over by the Scots and English, the road eventually reaches the small Northumbrian village of Cornhill on Tweed, the last settlement in England before crossing into Scotland. Although small, Cornhill has a rugged attractiveness in keeping with the region's history and the sturdy independence of its people.

A mile and a half on from Cornhill a sweeping right-hand curve brings into view a stone-built, five-arch bridge. Dating back to 1766, this structure crosses the River Tweed and marks the border between England and Scotland. After crossing the bridge, on the far side of which is a small cottage where for many years marriages were conducted, the road bears left to enter Coldstream, the Border town wherein Her Majesty's foot guards bearing that name were raised by General Monk in 1659. Steeped in history, for hundreds of years invading armies from north and south of the border passed through the town to do battle with each other, the most notable occasion being in 1513 when the English army under Thomas Howard, Earl of Surrey, defeated the invading Scots led by King James IV at the Battle of Flodden. On a more peaceful mission it was here that the Scottish poet Robert Burns made his first excursion in England in 1759, describing the event in his diary thus: 'Coldstream – went over into England. Cornhill – glorious River Tweed, clear, majestic. Fine bridge.'

Today Coldstream and the surrounding areas are the focus for campers and caravanners, while thousands of tourists annually pass through the town on their way further north. Those who break their journey in the town can wander along its High Street flanked with shops and public buildings, before turning off to visit the imposing mansion The Hirsel, home of the late Lord Home.

Friday, 30 July 1982, was a sweltering day with the temperature climbing well into the eighties, a comparatively rare luxury across the Border region of England and Scotland. During the morning Susan Claire Maxwell, a pretty, dark-haired eleven-year-old who lived with her mother Elizabeth, stepfather Fordyce and her stepbrother and sister Tom and Jacqueline at the family farm on the outskirts of Cornhill, had been shopping in Coldstream with her mother. After lunch she began to feel bored although it was still early into the summer holiday. With only Jacqueline, who would celebrate her fifth birthday in five days' time, and three-year-old Tom to play with in the garden, Susan telephoned her schoolfriend Alison Raeburn's Coldstream home and arranged to meet her later that afternoon for a game at the Lennel Tennis Club not far from Alison's home; Susan had only joined the club the previous week.

She asked her mother if she could cycle the mile and a half to her friend's home, but Elizabeth Maxwell was not keen on the idea, concerned at the prospect of her daughter cycling along the A697, crowded at that time of the year with holiday traffic but especially so on that particular Friday with people travelling to the annual Kelso show. Instead she persuaded Susan to take the safer option and walk to and from Coldstream.

Although not very happy at the prospect of walking into town in the heat of the afternoon, Susan Maxwell went indoors and changed, emerging a few minutes later wearing a yellow T-shirt with a palm tree motif on the front, matching shorts and white ankle socks and tennis shoes. A little while later she was about to depart carrying her racket, a ball and a flask of orange juice when John White, one of the farm workers who was about to drive into Coldstream, readily agreed to give her a lift.

The two of them arrived in Coldstream a few minutes early for Susan's meeting with her friend, so she wandered into the Tweed Garage where she was known. There was time to run a short errand to the nearby post office to buy some stamps for Mrs Home, the lady on duty, before going on to meet Alison.

The two eleven-year-olds met up and made their way happily to the tennis club where they spent the next hour playing tennis. Finally at the end of a set that Susan won by six games to five, the two of them left to walk back to their homes. They parted at the end of Lennel Mount, arranging to see each other the following Sunday at the Girl Guide parade being held as part of the opening of Coldstream's civic week.

Back at Cramond Hill farm, Elizabeth Maxwell, conscious that it was her daughter's first trip alone into Coldstream, and anticipating that she would be feeling hot and tired after her game, decided to drive into the town to meet her.

Elizabeth set off and drove to the tennis club, only to find it locked up with no sign of her daughter. She called at Alison Raeburn's address but was told by Mrs Raeburn that Alison also had not yet arrived home. After briefly touring the neighbourhood, Elizabeth Maxwell returned home without having come across her daughter. A few minutes later the telephone rang. It was Mrs Raeburn to say that Alison was back home, having parted from Susan outside Coldstream police station. Alison had last seen her friend walking towards Cornhill.

Despite the heat Elizabeth Maxwell felt a chill as she sought out her husband; Fordyce was equally concerned, sharing with his wife the conviction that Susan would not have accepted a lift from a stranger.

Within minutes of receiving the telephone call from the distraught-sounding Elizabeth Maxwell reporting that her eleven-year-old daughter Susan had not returned home from a game of tennis in Coldstream, the police at Cornhill and Coldstream realised that there was genuine cause for concern over the apparent disappearance of the sensible, level-headed schoolgirl.

A preliminary search of the area around where Susan Maxwell had last been seen was carried out the same evening, but it was not until the next morning that a full-scale search was mounted. Teams of policemen from both sides of the border, many with tracker dogs, set about searching an ever-widening area of open countryside, including the banks of the River Tweed. They were soon joined by Fordyce Maxwell and local volunteers, all of whom were equally concerned at the disappearance of their young neighbour.

While the search was going on, police were also making house-to-house inquiries in Coldstream, and were trying to trace anyone who may have seen Susan Maxwell walking home, or indeed anything that may have struck them as suspicious. Several people, including a woman who worked in a Cornhill garage, and a lorry driver who had stopped for a break on the English side of Coldstream bridge, were certain that the colourfully dressed schoolgirl had *not* passed them during the crucial minutes after she had parted from Alison Raeburn. The last positive sighting had been made by a Yorkshire businessman who had also stopped on the English side of the bridge.

Other people spoke of seeing a white van in the locality, at one time parked in a field gateway leading off the A697. Although there had been several sightings of the vehicle, with only a limited description, for the time being at least it was impossible to trace.

Later in the day Elizabeth Maxwell's father arrived from his home in Fife; after trying to reassure his daughter he left for home, having arranged to return on Tuesday with her mother.

On the second day of the search, Superintendent Jim Forster of the Northumbria Police, together with Detective Chief Inspector Fred Stephenson and Detective Inspector Andrew Farquhar of the Lothian and Borders force, called upon experienced fell rescue teams, and drafted in a Special Patrol Group and a team of crack divers from the National Police Diving School in Sunderland to bolster the search.

On Sunday the quest intensified as fear that Susan Maxwell had been abducted increased with each hour that passed. At Morning Prayer a packed congregation of villagers at the parish church of St Helen's joined the Reverend Arthur Wiltshire in prayer for their neighbours, and for the safe return of their daughter.

While hundreds of policemen and women, specialised detachments and civilian volunteers continued to scour the dense undergrowth that carpeted much of the search area, Superintendent Forster appealed for news of an old purple-coloured Mini Traveller that had been seen parked a short distance on the English side of Coldstream bridge between 4.30 p.m. and 4.45 p.m. on the afternoon Susan had gone missing. Witnesses spoke of seeing three youths, one of Asian appearance, another with a beard and wearing glasses, and the third with ginger hair, apparently picnicking near the vehicle.

Back at Cramond Hill farm, with her husband out with the search parties from dawn until dusk, Elizabeth Maxwell was trying for the sake of her two other children to maintain as normal a routine as possible. Both of them naturally missed their sister, Jacqueline especially so as she was looking forward to her fifth birthday party on the Wednesday and had been expecting Susan to be there, together with her cousins and friends.

Although she was outwardly calm, a hint of the turmoil within Elizabeth Maxwell was revealed when she told reporters, 'We have heard nothing. I am more certain than ever she [Susan] has been abducted. I think she has been taken in a car by someone she thought she knew. She could be anywhere . . .' Her fears were echoed by Superintendent Forster: 'We are getting calls from all over the country. But we are still appealing to anyone who was on the road between 4 p.m. and 5 p.m. to contact us.'

By Tuesday, 3 August, four days after Susan had gone missing, the massive search had failed to turn up a single clue as to what had happened to her. Jim Forster was clearly disappointed at the lack of progress: 'You would think that if Susan had gone missing in this area something would have turned up by now . . . but we have had nothing.'

On Tuesday afternoon Stanley Bailey, Northumbria's Chief Constable, made a morale-boosting visit to the police incident room at Cornhill during which he announced that at a public meeting that evening he would be asking the 300 villagers to agree to a house-to-house search. Later Detective Chief Inspector Stephenson expanded on the Chief Constable's reasoning: 'The child was heading towards her village home and I want to clear this village from the inquiry. When the search is completed here it may even have to be carried out in Coldstream where it will be an even greater task, but will be done with the assistance of the Lothian and Borders Police.'

Also on Tuesday Elizabeth Maxwell's parents were welcomed from Scotland; their presence was to do much to support the family in the days ahead.

That evening the audience in a packed village hall heard Andrew Easton, Chairman of Cornhill Parish Council, endorse fully the proposed house-to-house search: 'We are fully behind the police in their efforts to find Susan,' he said.

DCI Stephenson told villagers, 'We now feel we have searched the area thoroughly – as far as we can go. We come now to the private thing – your own homes. Can we go into your gardens, along your hedges and into your outhouses?' He encouraged people to search their own houses to eliminate the possibility that unbeknown to them their children had brought home some item belonging to Susan that they had found.

The result of the appeal was overwhelming; every home, shop and other building in Cornhill was opened for inspection by officers from the hundred-strong team allotted to the task. The message spread much further afield, owners of holiday homes in the area contacted police from various parts of the country giving their permission for their property to be searched in their absence, explaining when necessary how access could be gained. After two days with nothing discovered, Cornhill was eliminated from the inquiry.

During the days following Susan's disappearance, the feelings of Elizabeth and Fordyce Maxwell swung between optimism and despair. The unceasing police efforts to find their daughter encouraged them in the belief that if she was lying undiscovered in the surrounding countryside, or had ended up in the river, sooner or later her body would be found. On the other hand the lack of success somehow fostered the hope that Susan was alive and being held somewhere against her will.

Elizabeth and Fordyce had met when both were working as journalists. After they were married Fordyce had given up journalism for farming and the couple, together with Susan who was Elizabeth's daughter from her first marriage, had moved into Cramond Hill farm which Fordyce now worked with his brothers.

Fordyce had always lived near Cornhill and believed he knew intimately every wood, thicket and quarry within miles. Nevertheless, when he and his three brothers joined Special Patrol Group 'D' under Sergeant Hall, he quickly became aware of areas of the countryside with which even he was unfamiliar. The team covered several square miles each day, no one more diligently than Fordyce. His wife matched his effort in her own way back at the farm, her calm outward demeanour concealing the heartache and feelings of loneliness and despair she felt as she waited for news. Her stoicism was amply demonstrated on her daughter Jacqueline's birthday.

A party was to be held at Green Lane Cottage, the home of Jacqueline's grandmother less than a mile away from Cramond Hill farm. Mrs Alice Maxwell was arranging a barbecue for her granddaughter and her cousins and friends for which Susan had promised to bake a birthday cake topped with Smarties. With recent events overshadowing all else, the cake could have easily been overlooked. Not by Elizabeth Maxwell; aware of the sadness being felt by Jacqueline and Tom, Elizabeth was determined that her own feelings should not add to their unhappiness.

When Alice Maxwell had informed her daughter-in-law that she was arranging a birthday party for Jacqueline, Elizabeth baked a chocolate cake covered in white icing and topped with five red candles. She took it to the party along with a toy cash till which she told Jacqueline was a present from the family, including Susan. For the remainder of the afternoon the two women, together with Elizabeth's mother Cecilia Duncan, joined wholeheartedly in the birthday fun.

By Thursday, 5 August, nearly a week had elapsed since Susan Maxwell's disappearance. With the widespread search having so far proved unsuccessful, consideration was being given to new initiatives. The previous day it had been intended to charter a helicopter equipped with a thermal heat-seeking camera; it was planned that the aircraft should sweep across the Border countryside in the hope that the camera would reveal the location of Susan's body. Unfortuntely the plan had to be postponed due to the excessively hot weather which would have prevented the camera's effective use. Instead a Sea King helicopter from RAF Boulmer was called in to carry out a visual scan of the area.

While the helicopter clattered across the countryside, seven dog handlers from a Scottish mountain rescue team whose animals were specially trained to seek out human bodies lost in difficult terrain, reinforced those searching on the ground.

On both sides of the border the police search was unremitting. Chief Superintendent Grant Till of the Lothian and Borders Police, when reporting that house-to-house inquiries in Coldstream had been completed, announced that a house-to-house search was to be carried out similar to that at Cornhill. He pointed out that such a task in Coldstream presented far greater problems than in the village where there were only about eighty houses. Meanwhile in Northumbria, Superintendent Forster appealed to 152 equestrians taking part in the annual Coldstream to Flodden Field commemorative ride to keep a look-out for any clues to Susan Maxwell's disappearance.

On Thursday detectives introduced an unusual tactic. Elizabeth Maxwell was invited to the police incident room in Cornhill village hall to watch a two-minute school video film showing her daughter reading a poem in her classroom. Senior detectives had considered the matter carefully before deciding to suggest the idea to Mrs Maxwell, balancing the emotional effect it may have had against the possible benefit. In the event Susan's mother enjoyed seeing and hearing her daughter on film, and agreed to it being showed nationwide on networked television the following evening in the hope that it would encourage anyone with information to contact the police. 'I know it's only a film but it seems as though she was still there . . .' was Elizabeth Maxwell's verdict afterwards.

Again in the hope of stirring people's memories, on Friday afternoon Susan Jackson, the twelve-year-old daughter of a lorry driver and a Susan Maxwell lookalike, dressed herself in clothes similar to those the missing girl had been wearing and retraced her likely route from Coldstream the previous week. At the same time Northumbria Police mounted a road block on the English side of Coldstream bridge during which they interviewed two drivers who had passed along that stretch of the A697 about the same time the week before. 'This reconstruction has been well worth while,' said DCI Stephenson.

The response to both initiatives bore this out. Dozens of telephone calls were logged and recorded at the Northumbrian incident room where they were analysed and appropriate follow-up action was put in hand. Inspector John Patterson, the Northumbrian Police press officer, voiced official appreciation of the response: 'We have received countless calls from all over the country . . . it is all to be digested. All the information is useful; it helps us to pin things down and build up a picture of what might have happened.'

He went on to explain that the two forces involved north and south of the border had widened their search and were now 'making in-depth searches of particular places'.

A week had passed since Susan Maxwell had disappeared during the short walk between Coldstream and her Cornhill home. Already hundreds of acres of Border countryside had been carefully searched, both on the ground and from the air. Scores of people had been questioned during house-to-house inquiries and at road checks. Details of the incident and police appeals had been widely shown on television, and there had been extensive coverage of the story and day-to-day progress reports in national and local newspapers.

Despite this massive effort and wide media coverage, police were no nearer discovering Susan's whereabouts or what had happened to her than they had been on the day she had gone missing. Hours spent crawling along sewers, struggling through waist-high, nettle-choked undergrowth, probing cess pits, combing the banks of the River Tweed and wading through countless ponds and streams, had all failed to produce a single lead.

Among the many interviews carried out by the police were those of Fordyce Maxwell and John White, the farm worker who had given Susan a lift into Coldstream. Neither of them was suspected of involvement, but both found the experience traumatic. It is to their credit that neither man objected to the police questions, accepting that it was a part of the investigation designed to eliminate them from the inquiry.

Detectives were still anxious to trace the three young men who had been seen picnicking near Coldstream bridge. Several people who had spoken to them had come forward and added to the sum of knowledge about them. From what they had said it seemed they were from Tyneside and may have been going north in their 1972 or 1973 Mini Traveller to seek fruit-picking work in the Blairgowrie area of Perthshire.

At Cramond Hill farm, Elizabeth Maxwell was immersing herself in housework; washing, ironing and spring cleaning while all the time hoping that Susan would be found safe and unharmed. 'I just won't let myself think the worst,' she said. 'It's the fact that there's been no news at all, no clues whatsoever, that makes it so terrible . . . Someone must surely have her, have seen her.' Although still determined to find her, police secretly now had grave doubts that Susan Maxwell was still alive.

The Maxwell family, villagers and a number of police officers at Sunday's Morning Prayer heard the Reverend Arthur Wiltshire say, 'Our everyday way of life, which to some people may seem very ordinary, has been under attack in a way none of us has ever experienced. For some inexplicable reason Susan has been taken from us . . . the police were seeking a sign which would lead them to Susan, but had no clue about what had happened to her . . . Why it has happened I do not know. I cannot give any reason for it.' The clergyman's bewilderment was shared by all those who were present. DCI Stephenson later described the service as 'emotional', and pointed out that many of the officers involved in the search had children of their own and felt natural empathy with the family.

That evening Detective Inspector Tony Furzeland of the Devon and Cornwall Constabulary travelled up to Northumbria at the invitation of the local force. DI Furzeland had spent four years investigating the disappearance of thirteen-year-old Genette Tate who vanished in August 1978 while delivering newspapers in a country lane near Exeter. It was thought that the experience gained by DI Furzeland over the four years would benefit the Maxwell case, if only by helping the Northumbrian detectives avoid any mistakes that had occurred during the West Country inquiry.

On Monday morning DI Furzeland accompanied DCI Stephenson on a visit to the scene of Susan Maxwell's disappearance. Later they toured the surrounding area before finally having a discussion about the case with other senior Northumbrian officers. As the terrain that had been searched in Devon was similar to that of the Borders region, DI Furzeland suggested that the delayed air search now be implemented. While discounting any connection between the two inquiries, the West Country detective made further suggestions regarding the most effective search pattern and personnel deployment.

There was a sudden flurry of activity later on Monday when a police searcher brought a tramp to the incident room whom he had seen in possession of a blue flask similar to that which had been carried by Susan. However, hope of it being a useful lead disappeared after Elizabeth Maxwell had failed to identify the object. Police also issued a description of two American tourists they wished to trace. The two had been spotted taking photographs on Coldstream bridge on the day Susan disappeared, and detectives thought it conceivable that something useful would show up on the developed prints.

For the next two days efforts were stepped up to trace the three young men seen picnicking near Coldstream bridge. Over a dozen reported sightings of purple Minis had been received, mainly from the north of England, and on Wednesday a small squad of detectives went to Newcastle to follow up reports that the vehicle had been seen in the Tyneside region.

Back at Cornhill the Special Patrol Group had been increased to twenty-five officers, while detectives from Lothian and Borders, working alongside those from Northumbria, were joined by a number of police cadets whose task it was to take to canoes and further search the reeded banks of the Tweed near Coldstream.

On Thursday, with the inquiry almost two weeks old, the emphasis changed; until then it had been a missing person inquiry, but now police tacitly accepted that Susan Maxwell was no longer alive. Henceforth the inquiry became a full-scale murder investigation.

Another significant development that day saw an end of the search for the three men with the purple Mini. Following its return from Perthshire, Tyneside detectives had traced the vehicle. The occupants were interviewed at Newcastle and later made written statements. Soon afterwards all three were eliminated from the inquiry, DCI Stephenson announcing that 'The men have not been arrested' and had not helped to further the inquiry.

Friday, 13 August, two weeks exactly since Susan Maxwell had vanished on that hot summer afternoon. During that time police efforts had been unremitting. At one stage over 300 officers and scores of volunteers had been employed for sixteen hours a day. They had searched over 80 square miles of countryside, including every hedgerow and ditch along the 45-mile stretch of the A697 between Coldstream and Morpeth. Also, at the suggestion of Hector Clark, an Assistant Chief Constable of Northumbria who at the time was not actively involved in the investigation, policemen from Northumbria and Lothian and Borders searched every lay-by for 50 miles north and south of Coldstream. Everything from helicopters to canoes had been co-opted into the operation. House searches and road checks had been carried out as a result of which hundreds of drivers and other people were questioned. Over 500 written statements had been obtained. Despite everything, police were still no nearer discovering what had happened to Susan Maxwell.

Throughout this period Elizabeth and Fordyce Maxwell had been experiencing the anguish of waiting for news. They had continued to display the fortitude that had already earned them universal respect. Not once had either of them faltered in public, and each had given the police their unqualified support.

On that Friday, 13 August, Elizabeth Maxwell had a special appointment. She was due to appear on the Jimmy Young Radio 2 show to make a nationwide appeal for help in finding her daughter. Accompanied by DCI Stephenson, she travelled to the BBC Radio Newcastle satellite studio at Alnwick Castle. There she told listeners that 'The only explanation left is that she [Susan] had been persuaded to get into someone's car and gone away somewhere, and someone is holding her prisoner against her will . . . We feel that if there had been a road accident or anything of that description something would have turned up.'

DCI Stephenson told Mr Young: 'This person may be in need of help . . . We ask that they release Susan and direct her to the nearest police station.'

The interviewer then added his own plea: 'If you were in the area and even think you know something, for goodness sake contact the police right away.'

At the end of the programme Mrs Maxwell was driven back to Cramond Hill farm, wondering whether her appeal may have touched a chord among the millions of people who had tuned into the programme. Tragically it was not to be.

Less than an hour after Elizabeth Maxwell had arrived home there was a knock at the front door. She opened it to see again DCI Stephenson, this time accompanied by several of his colleagues. When they were inside the policeman turned to Mrs Maxwell.

'I've had the police at Uttoxeter on the phone,' he told her. 'They have found a little girl. This little girl is not alive.' The search for Susan Maxwell was over.

CHAPTER 5

'I THINK IT COULD BE HER'

August 1982–July 1983

Arthur Meadows could not believe his eyes. It was Thursday, 12 August 1982, and the thirty-year-old Uttoxeter lorry driver had pulled into a lay-by on the A518 Uttoxeter to Stafford road intending to call at a friend's house nearby to borrow a CB radio before continuing his journey to Scotland. To reach the house he was taking a short cut through a small wood when he passed a shallow depression in the ground.

'I glanced down to the left and was absolutely frozen with fear,' he told police later. 'I saw a pair of white socks, I thought it must have been a dummy.' Hastening to his friend's house, a shaken Meadows collected the radio, omitting to mention what he had seen a short while before.

On the drive to Scotland Arthur Meadows had ample time to mull over the situation. He tried to convince himself that it had been a dummy lying in the wood, but doubt persisted. Soon after he arrived at his destination he confided in another driver who advised him immediately to inform the police. Still unconvinced, Meadows nevertheless complied with the suggestion and telephoned the police back at Uttoxeter.

Detective Inspector Peter Herward was one of the first policemen to arrive at the scene later that evening. 'We looked at the body which was obviously that of a young child. The local Chief Inspector who had with him a telex of missing persons said, "I think it could be her." However, it was the next day before we were able to make a positive identification by means of things like clothing, fingerprints and dental records. That started it all off.' Little did Peter Herward realise, as he stood that night in the wood looking down at the small body, that for the next twelve years a large part of his professional life was to be devoted to the search for the little girl's killer.

A brief preliminary examination carried out by torchlight revealed little more than that, apart from the shoes, the body appeared to be fully clothed. The wood was then cordoned off until a more detailed examination could be made in daylight.

Meanwhile, during the night, DI Peter Herward and other detectives drove up to Scotland and brought Arthur Meadows back to Staffordshire. Having failed to report his find immediately to the police, Meadows early on found himself under suspicion. He later explained in a written statement: 'I tried to tell myself it was a dummy I had seen and not a body. It had frightened me. I was still shaky when I got to my friend's house.'

Questioned about his whereabouts on Friday, 30 July, Meadows was at first completely unable to recall where he had been. Eventually he remembered that he had in fact been on holiday, and was able to catalogue all the people he had spoken to on that day. Teams of policemen soon traced enough of these to enable them to eliminate Meadows from the inquiry. His relief was inexpressible; tears flowed, and it was much later before he felt able to fully discuss his experience.

It has long been accepted police practice that the lead in a murder inquiry is taken by the force in whose area the body is found. This procedure, perverse as it may appear, is adopted as traditionally in a joint investigation the force which harbours the most serious offence heads the inquiry. This was the arrangement in the Susan Maxwell case with Detective Chief Superintendent Derek Boden, the deputy head of Staffordshire CID, deputed to take charge of the investigation.

The day after Susan Maxwell's body was found was one of hectic activity. The wood in which she had lain had already been taped off, and as soon as it was light police photographers and forensic experts together with scene of crime officers attended the scene while dozens of uniformed and CID officers trawled through the undergrowth looking for clues. By the time the search had been completed an estimated 40 tons of rubbish had been shifted from the site. DCS Boden pointed out that the wood had for a long time been used as a rubbish dump. During the days that followed members of the public regularly came forward with information and details regarding sightings of people near the wood. All these were followed up, but disappointingly nothing of value emerged.

Early on that first day a police incident room manned by Staffordshire officers was set up at Uttoxeter police station. Later a satellite room was opened at the police station at Coldstream. This was staffed by men and women, including civilians, of Staffordshire, Northumbria and the

Lothian and Borders Police, with a detective inspector from each force appointed to liaise with his opposite numbers and co-ordinate the inquiries. The system worked well and heralded the greater co-operation between constabularies that was to characterise future, much larger inquiries.

DI Herward was to be the Staffordshire liaison officer assigned to Coldstream. Himself a family man, he told me that at the time he was in Scotland his own daughter, also called Susan, 'was just a wee bit younger than Susie Maxwell; it really brought it home to me'. Similar feelings were frequently expressed to me by officers engaged in the investigation, family men in particular feeling a deep personal involvement in the inquiry.

A development on Friday afternoon gave rise to hope of an early break-through. Mark Ball, a young psychiatric nurse, contacted detectives and told them that having just listened to Elizabeth Maxwell's appeal on the Jimmy Young show, he had some information that he thought might be of value. He said that on 30 July, the day that Susan had vanished, he had been driving south along the A697 when he had seen a girl about Susan Maxwell's age struggling with a man who was in the front passenger seat of a maroon-coloured Triumph 2000 motor car; at the same time she appeared to be striking the side of the vehicle with a tennis racket.

Detectives regarded the sighting as crucial, and a plan was immediately set in hand to trace and interview the owners of all maroon Triumph 2000s. It was a mammoth undertaking in which thousands of posters were distributed, by the end of which over 19,000 had been seen.

However, there was not complete unanimity among the investigating officers regarding the likely involvement of the suspect vehicle. DI Herward was one who was unable to reconcile the time of Susan Maxwell's disappearance at 4.10 p.m. with the established sighting of the car at about 4.55 p.m. Why was there such a time discrepancy, he asked. Hector Clark, who the following year was to take overall charge of the inquiry, also doubted the veracity of the sighting. He queried why, in view of the massive publicity surrounding Susan Maxwell's disappearance, Mark Ball had delayed so long before contacting the police. These doubts expressed by senior detectives were vindicated when involvement of the vehicle in Susan's abduction was eventually discounted.

A post-mortem examination also carried out that Friday morning at Burton-on-Trent failed to reveal the cause of death, but indicated that Susan's body had been dumped soon after she had gone missing.

News of the discovery provoked the inevitable public outcry. Horror, alarm and calls for retribution dominated newspaper and television reports with Mr Ivan Lawrence, the MP for Burton, leading a fresh demand for the restoration of capital punishment.

During the days immediately following the discovery of Susan Maxwell's body, the police intensified their investigation. Transport firms with links between Scotland and the Midlands were contacted and drivers questioned; caravan sites within a 10-mile radius of Coldstream were visited; hotels in or near Uttoxeter and Coldstream provided details of people who had recently been on holiday in the hope that they might have useful information. Shops and businesses in Staffordshire, the Borders and Northumbria were visited. Efforts were made to trace commercial travellers and others who may have stayed overnight near Uttoxeter, and Scottish-based oil workers who had spent the weekend at their homes in the Midlands were sought out.

The Staffordshire Police were soon faced with an administrative nightmare, its database alone eventually containing half a million index cards. A card index system was in use until the introduction of computers following the abduction and murder of Caroline Hogg in 1983. In the meantime in the Uttoxeter incident room 116,000 entries were card-recorded on the vehicle index, while a further 17,000 cards related to statements.

On Sunday, 15 August there had come news of a nine-year-old boy having been found clubbed to death near his home at Ripon in North Yorkshire. The body was lying 5 miles from the A1, the road along which it was believed Susan Maxwell's abductor had travelled on his way south. Because of the similarities between the two cases – both victims were children and both had been bound up before death – detectives from Yorkshire met their Staffordshire counterparts to establish whether or not the two cases were linked; within twenty-four hours the possibility had been ruled out.

On the same day the Reverend Peter Miln led prayers for Susan Maxwell, her family and the detectives seeking her killer.

Midway through the first week DCS Boden travelled to Northumbria where he retraced Susan Maxwell's last walk. Later, together with Northumbrian officers, he visited Elizabeth and Fordyce Maxwell. 'I feel and hope they appreciated the visit . . . They are anxious to help us in any way possible,' he said later. Over the years reciprocal visits were to continue to take place between detectives from the different forces.

On Thursday similar clothing to that worn by Susan Maxwell at the time she went missing was put on display at Uttoxeter police station, while photographs of her wearing the distinctive T-shirt and yellow shorts were displayed throughout the region in the hope that someone would recall having seen her.

Twelve days after her body had been found Mr Edward Huntback, the East Staffordshire coroner sitting at Uttoxeter, opened the inquest into Susan Maxwell's death. DCS Boden told Mr Huntback that 'The body was extremely difficult to identify, so much so we had to rely on dental and fingerprint evidence.' He admitted that the cause of death was still not known, and explained that more forensic tests had still to be carried out. Without calling further witnesses, the coroner expressed the hope that the investigation would 'bear fruit', before adjourning the inquest to a future date to be set.

While detectives from the Midlands, Scotland and the north-east continued to pursue different lines of inquiry, on Saturday, 28 August, over 250 miles away in the parish churchyard of St Helen's in Cornhill, Susan Claire Maxwell, described by the Reverend Arthur Wiltshire as 'a gem of a little girl, whom it was always a joy to meet', was finally laid to rest. Over 500 mourners, including several of the senior investigating officers, attended the service. As Susan was interred with her favourite teddy bear, Elizabeth and Fordyce kissed a single red rose before dropping it in to rest on top of her coffin.

As the weeks and months passed, hundreds of lines of inquiry were followed up. Men against whom there was only slight suspicion were seen and interviewed before they were eliminated from the inquiry. Vehicles spotted at or near Coldstream or Uttoxeter that may have had a link with the crime were traced wherever possible, while a mass of assorted information that required investigation was either dealt with at Uttoxeter or passed on to the incident room at Coldstream.

Although there was disapointment at the lack of a breakthrough, complete co-operation existed between detectives from Staffordshire, Northumbria and Lothian and Borders. Occasionally a sense of frustration was felt by Northumbrian officers within whose area Susan Maxwell had been abducted, at the initiative in the inquiry having been taken by Staffordshire. As Detective Sergeant (later Detective Chief Inspector) Dennis Cleugh, who as a member of the Northumbria Police crime squad was involved in the Robert Black case from its outset, recalls:

Although Northumbria retained a satellite incident room based at Coldstream, this seemed to lose the 'positive aspect' in some aspects as the SIO [senior investigating officer] had no real allegiance to the area of abduction. Nevertheless, I personally formed a strong, lasting and I believe professional relationship with many operational officers from other forces who all had the same objective in mind.

In October 1982, DCS Boden announced that detectives were keen to interview a teenage cyclist spotted near the scene of Susan Maxwell's abduction at about the time she went missing. A witness said the rider had been 'looking over his shoulder and wobbling all over the place', and it was thought possible that he may have seen Susan being taken. Police also wanted to trace a red car seen emerging from a field known as 'Peter's Plantation' on the A697 at roughly the same time. Nothing resulted from either appeal.

During the spring of 1983, with no arrest likely, the inquiry gradually tailed off. In April the Coldstream incident room was closed down; thereafter inquiries in Scotland or Northumbria were sent direct to the appropriate force. Three months later the Staffordshire incident room in Uttoxeter was transferred to the Adams biscuit factory nearby, thereby allowing the police station to resume a more normal routine. Although the inquiry had been scaled down, there remained a sizeable contingent of detectives engaged on the Maxwell investigation.

That was the situation prevailing when, in July 1983, five-year-old Caroline Hogg was kidnapped from the sea front at Portobello near Edinburgh. Ten days later on Monday, 18 July, DCS Boden told assembled Staffordshire detectives that the body of a little girl, believed to be that of Caroline Hogg, had been found in a ditch by a lay-by in Leicestershire. Instinctively those present knew that the predator they had been seeking for a whole year had struck again.

Peter Herward: 'What had we done? Had we omitted doing anything which might have prevented the latest murder? There was nothing at all. We had given total commitment to it for twelve months, and now we were faced with another one.' There was depression all round.

CHAPTER 6

SNATCHED AT THE SEASIDE

July 1983

Caroline Hogg had enjoyed her afternoon at a friend's birthday party. Wearing her favourite lilac and white gingham dress, her party shoes, and with her blonde hair held back in two bunches, the five-year-old had eaten her fill of cakes and ice-cream before excitedly joining in the fun and games.

The afternoon of Friday, 8 July 1983 had passed quickly for the little girl and to her it seemed all too soon that her mother arrived to collect her. When they arrived home Caroline was pleased to see that her nana was there. Although it was nearing tea-time Annette Hogg agreed that her daughter could go out and play for half an hour providing as always that she did not wander beyond the limits that her mother and stepfather had set for her close to home.

Caroline came indoors a few minutes late for her tea. Having had her fill of party fare earlier she wasn't feeling hungry; instead she wanted to go back outside to play. However, as none of her friends were about the little girl was content instead to accompany her mother and nana the few hundred yards to Portobello High Street where her grandmother caught a bus home.

Although it was nearly seven o'clock by the time Annette and her daughter arrived back at 25 Beach Lane, it was still a pleasantly warm, sunny evening with crowds sauntering along the mile-long Portobello promenade, some of them enjoying the amusements that flanked it. Nevertheless, when Caroline pleaded again to be allowed to stay out and play, her mother was firm. No, it was too late and past her bedtime. Undeterred by this response, Caroline turned to her step-daddy. Like many fathers with pretty, beguiling five-year-old daughters, John Hogg succumbed to her blandishments and agreed that she could go out for another five minutes; first she must change out of her party shoes, and under no circumstances was she to go beyond the garden gate. Caroline happily agreed, changing from her party shoes into a pair of incongruous-looking pink trainers before running out through the front door.

Earlier that day in Uttoxeter, the coroner, Mr Edward Huntback, had recorded an open verdict at the adjourned inquest into Susan Maxwell's death. The inquest had heard from Dr Scholz van der Merwe, the Home Office pathologist, that Susan's body had lain in the wood off the A518 for at least ten days. Although he was able to state that she had not been sexually assaulted, and that no bones were broken, he had been unable to establish the cause of death.

Three miles east of Edinburgh city centre lies its less illustrious seaside neighbour. Portobello, at one time a major Victorian resort but now with a much-reduced aesthetic appeal, still attracts visitors from Scotland's capital and the surrounding region. Its sands and mile-long promenade with bars and amusements overlooking the Firth of Forth are its principal attractions, appealing to young and old, especially during the summer when its population is substantially increased by holiday-makers and day trippers.

The resort (one irritates its inhabitants by referring to it as a suburb of Edinburgh) is bisected by the High Street and Abercorn Terrace. To the north of these a dozen or more streets run at right angles down to the sea front, while on the south lie several Georgian terraces and crescents, Sir Harry Lauder Road, named after Portobello's most celebrated son, and the public golf course.

Beach Lane, where John and Annette Hogg lived with their five children in a semi-detached Victorian villa, is one of the streets that lead on to the promenade. The houses, many of which are spacious enough to have been converted into flats and bed-sits, are still dwarfed by the three-storeyed Towerbank primary school which overshadows the area. John and Annette's home faced the school playground, while at the rear lay a housing estate.

As the lively five-year-old went out into the small front garden that evening, her father's strict injunction to stay close to home was almost immediately forgotten. The sight and sound of the holiday-makers, swings in the small park by her school, the promenade with its myriad attractions (not to mention the perils) and the sea, glistening and sparkling in the evening sunlight beyond the sea wall, proved irresistible.

After playing perfunctorily for a few minutes on the swings, Caroline wandered further down Beach Lane to the promenade where she was soon swallowed up in the crowd. It is not known exactly how or where she met Robert Black; it was established later that earlier that Friday Black had made a poster delivery just over a mile away at the Mills and Allen depot in Piershall Terrace. Since then several children had noticed a scruffy-looking man hanging about in the area near the sea front. Seventeen-year-old Laura McPherson made the most significant sighting. She spotted Caroline on the promenade laughing happily in company with a stranger.

Caroline Hogg was last seen alive about 7.30 p.m. by a children's round-about attendant at the Fun City amusement park. Derek Jackson, who was also seventeen, later told police how he had seen Caroline, whom he knew, enter the fairground holding the hand of a man who then paid 15p for her to have a ride on the carousel's double-decker bus. Afterwards he watched the pair, still holding hands, walk off towards the car-park.

It had turned half-past seven when Annette Hogg decided that it was time for Caroline to come indoors. She had already been out longer than John Hogg had agreed, but Annette was not too concerned at this stage as it was a warm evening and her daughter was enjoying herself so much that day . . .

From the front door Annette called Caroline but there was no reply. She was certain that the little girl was not far away: had she not repeatedly drummed into her that she must never go by herself to the swings, the beach, the funfair or the amusement arcades? Her mother was certain that Caroline would not risk being smacked as she had been once before when she had wandered off alone to the park.

She was probably at the back of the house where her eleven-year-old brother Stuart was kicking a football around with a few of his pals. No, he hadn't seen Caroline, Stuart told his mother. Annette felt the first stir-rings of unease; if her daughter was not close to home, where was she? She went back into the house and told her husband that there was no sign of Caroline. John Hogg, conscious that it was he who had allowed the little girl to go out for the extra few minutes, hurried down to the prom-enade to look for her and call her name, but there was still no sign of her.

Back at Beach Lane Annette and Stuart were searching the immediate neighbourhood; looking over garden walls, calling out and checking other places to which Caroline may have wandered. By now the Hoggs were becoming increasingly worried. Telling their other children to carry on looking for their sister, they called on neighbours to help with the search. Word soon spread that the five-year-old could not be found, and soon a posse of friends and neighbours had joined the family in combing the area.

When a little boy approached Annette Hogg and told her that he had seen Caroline with a man on the promenade, her fear changed to dread. Immediately all the searchers turned their attention to the sea front. They mingled with the crowd, scouring through the funfair and amusement arcades, but their efforts stayed fruitless. Where was she? With hundreds of people still thronging the promenade, Fun City and the arcades, it would be easy to miss seeing even such a distinctively dressed child. The unthinkable, that Caroline had gone off somewhere with a stranger, was looming ever larger in everyone's minds.

By 8.30 p.m., nearly an hour after Annette Hogg had gone to fetch her daughter in for bed, it was decided that the situation was now beyond neighbourly resources and that it was time the police were informed.

It is doubtful if any Lothian and Borders policeman or woman was unaware of the Susan Maxwell inquiry in which for the past year their force had been so heavily involved; many of them would have helped in the search for Susan. So, when an agitated Annette Hogg telephoned Portobello police station to report that her five-year-old daughter was missing, alarm bells rang in their minds immediately. No time was lost; in less than an hour fifty uniformed officers had been mustered and deployed to search the area, and an urgent message had been sent to Detective Chief Superintendent Brian Cunningham, the head of Lothian and Borders CID, informing him of the situation.

Marion Rodgers from Portobello still vividly remembers the day that Caroline Hogg went missing:

> I had left my own children on the beach each with an ice-cream, and with strict instructions not to move away, while I went to collect a rabbit hutch. After taking the hutch home I went back and collected the children. That evening I noticed a large number of policemen about, looking through garages, sheds and gardens. I found out later that they were searching for Caroline Hogg. Believe me, it was a most salutary experience.

The police search witnessed by Marion Rodgers continued well into that first night, but without finding a trace of the missing girl. By daybreak it was radiating away from the Portobello beach area. Within two hours of Annette Hogg telephoning the police, the press were aware of the situation. Although the media are frequently criticised for their sensational reporting of murder cases, it must be acknowledged that during the investigation into the abduction and killing of Susan Maxwell, Caroline Hogg and Sarah Harper, newspaper and television coverage with few exceptions was restrained and constructive, on several occasions being of positive help to the authorities.

Helpful local reporting on the day following Caroline's disappearance prompted nearly 600 people to converge on Portobello within three days to help those already engaged in the search. On Sunday her disappearance was headline news in the national papers with comparison already being made between the latest disappearance and that of Susan Maxwell twelve months earlier. The similarities between the two cases was to become increasingly apparent as time passed.

What of John and Annette Hogg during this harrowing period? Both stayed out of the public gaze, making only a brief television appeal and keeping contact with the press to a minimum. Understandably while awaiting news of their daughter they preferred to rely upon the support of close friends and relations.

Certainly the search mounted for Caroline Hogg in the summer of 1983, co-ordinated from Leith and Portobello police stations, was comparable to that carried out a year before on the Borders. A little boy, one of several children who had noticed an unkempt man hanging about that evening, told police he had seen Caroline, whom he knew, looking frightened while walking hand-in-hand with a scruffy-looking stranger wearing thick-lensed glasses. It appears that Caroline was still in the vicinity of the promenade at the time that John and Annette Hogg were searching for her. Tragically their paths did not cross.

House-to-house inquiries and widespread police appeals soon produced other witnesses who remembered seeing the solitary little girl on the Friday evening making her way towards the sea front. Crucially, other people were traced who recalled seeing her with a man that evening; one person had spotted them near King's Road, less than a quarter of a mile from Beach Lane. Meanwhile, by the second weekend of the inquiry, over 2000 people had volunteered to help the police with the search which by now had extended as far as Edinburgh.

Mr Solly Macintosh, an arcade owner, informed police that two days before Caroline Hogg's disappearance he had become suspicious of a vagrant whom he had seen speaking to a young girl. The witness said that he had challenged the man who had then made off. The police succeeded in tracing this early suspect, but he satisfied them that he was unconnected with Caroline's disappearance.

Eventually a description was built up of the man seen on the Friday evening with the missing girl. Between 5 ft 8 ins and 5 ft 9 ins tall, well-built and wearing National Health-type horn-rimmed spectacles, he was said to be of a generally scruffy appearance and was dressed in a blue zip-up jacket and faded blue jeans. The description fitted thousands of men, but it was at least a start and enabled a police artist to draw up an impression of him. Although not immediately released to the press, this later proved to bear a close resemblance to Robert Black.

By the end of the first weekend an area of 15 square miles including several parks, golf courses and waste land around Portobello had been searched by the police and civilian volunteers. With the operation so widespread and involving hundreds of people, administrative problems arose, not least that of catering for so many. This particular difficulty was overcome when Portobello and District Community Association joined forces with local caterers to provide meals.

On Monday, 11 July fifty men from the Royal Scots Fusiliers were drafted in to help with the search which by then had moved to the centre of Edinburgh. While some teams of searchers combed the terrain within Holyrood Park and on Arthur's Seat, the hill overlooking the city, other groups moved in on Princes Street Gardens and Queen's Gardens; raking through bushes, hedges and shrubs, and targeting restaurants, gardeners' sheds and other structures where a body could have been dumped or hidden. City centre car-parks were thoroughly probed in case a child's body had lain somewhere undiscovered by shoppers or commuters.

During the time of this activity, dozens of telephone calls continued to be received at Portobello and Leith police stations where they were recorded, sifted and where appropriate acted upon. A police incident caravan was also set up at the Fun City amusement park to enable members of the public to speak personally to a police officer if they preferred. The caravan served also to reassure local people that police were doing everything they could think of in their effort to find out what had happened to Caroline Hogg.

It was the biggest search for a missing person ever mounted in Scotland. During the week over 2000 civilian volunteers and 140 policemen and women alone scoured Musselburgh racecourse and the

Blackford Hills. Superintendent Ronald Stalker later told a press conference at Portobello police station: 'I am afraid that all we have to say at
this stage is that we have turned up nothing at all . . . any child missing is
an emotive thing, and Portobello is a confined area. People have seen the
police activity during the week so it has been kept in their minds.'

It was still in the forefront of people's minds when on Monday, 18 July,
ten days after she had disappeared the news everyone had been fearing
arrived from the police in Leicestershire. Caroline Hogg's naked body
had been found over 300 miles away in a lay-by off the A444 near
Twycross, just 24 miles from where Susan Maxwell had been found.
Another search had ended.

CHAPTER 7

EL SUPREMO

It was with a mixture of relief and dejection that police officers involved in the search greeted the news that Caroline Hogg's body had been found in a Leicestershire lay-by. Relief that the uncertainty as to her fate was over, dejection at knowing that a child killer was on the loose. This applied particularly to those men who had been engaged on the Susan Maxwell inquiry and who suspected that the same man was responsible for both murders.

Caroline's body had been found by Gary Roberts, a sales executive, after he had pulled into the lay-by to relieve himself. As he had picked his way across the grass verge towards the ditch beyond, he had noticed 'a terrible smell'. Descending into the ditch Roberts had seen lying at the bottom the naked body of a little girl. Suppressing his personal need, he had scrambled out of the ditch, run to a nearby house and gasped out to the occupant what he had seen before telephoning the police.

The discovery of Caroline Hogg's body, and the linking almost immediately of her death with that of Susan Maxwell, heralded a new phase of the murder inquiry, one that was to continue until the conviction of Robert Black eleven years later.

Within hours of the latest discovery the Chief Constables of the forces investigating the crimes against Susan Maxwell and Caroline Hogg had made a far-reaching joint decision. Sir Stanley Bailey of Northumbria, Alan Goodson of Leicestershire, Charles Kelly of Staffordshire and William (later Sir William) Sutherland of Lothian and Borders concluded that there was in all likelihood a connection between the two cases, and that it would be expedient to appoint a senior investigating officer to co-ordinate the inquiries.

For the man selected it would present a formidable challenge. Answerable only to the four chief officers, he would be required to ensure that resources were deployed effectively, and would need to keep an eye on the economics of the inquiries. As he would be the public figurehead, the kudos would largely be his if there was a successful outcome; conversely, if success proved elusive he would be the principal target and would have to reply to criticism not only of himself, but of those working with him. Finally, he would have to handle the internecine feuding and jealousy that would inevitably accompany such an unprecedented appointment, which if not promptly and tactfully dealt with could jeopardise the entire enterprise.

It was decided that the man to be invited to take on this responsibility should be Hector Clark, the Assistant Chief Constable of Northumbria. Clark was a vastly experienced policeman who at the time of his appointment had twenty-eight years' service behind him, all of it in his native north-east. He had been a detective for all but four of those years and had been successfully involved in over seventy murder investigations.

Hector Clark is a big man. Standing over six feet and with shoulders to match, square-jawed and with ice-blue eyes that look appraisingly from under thick black eyebrows, he gives an immediate impression of a calculating and resolute investigator.

When his appointment was announced publicly the press lost no time in investing him with the title 'El Supremo', a soubriquet by which he became widely known by his colleagues. The only person who seems not to have been impressed with his appointment was his wife Anne. Asked by a reporter what she thought of it, she replied, 'He might be El Supremo to you, but I've still got to wash his socks!'

The day following the discovery of Caroline Hogg's body Detective Chief Superintendent David Baker, the head of Leicestershire CID, took upon himself the distressing duty of visiting her parents to verify her identity. He took with him to Edinburgh two hair bobbles and a silver locket that had been found on the little girl's body. That evening after John and Annette Hogg had identified the items, DCS Baker returned to Leicestershire with Caroline's dental records so that a final comparison could be made.

Meanwhile Hector Clark arrived in Edinburgh on Sunday to be met by Detective Chief Superintendent Brian Cunningham who had been in charge of the initial inquiry when Caroline Hogg had been reported missing, and then of the Edinburgh end when it had escalated into a full-scale murder investigation. Cunningham had already made a connection between the latest case and that of Susan Maxwell, speaking of the

'striking similarities' between them. More cautiously he had told reporters, 'Obviously there are things we have uppermost in our minds. A link
between the two has not been ruled out.' Clark had familiarised himself
with the Susan Maxwell case being investigated by Staffordshire and his
own force; Cunningham now filled in the details surrounding the abduction and murder of Caroline Hogg.

The Lothian and Borders chief told Clark among other things that they
were checking on a hundred or so reports of motor vehicles seen on the
A444 near Twycross, or at the lay-by near where Caroline Hogg had been
found. He went on to say that during the three days immediately preceding the anniversary of Susan Maxwell's disappearance on 30 July,
Lothian and Borders Police, in concert with Detective Chief
Superintendent Derek Boden of Staffordshire, were to set up a mobile
police station near Coldstream in the hope that the anniversary would stir
members of the public into coming forward with new information.

During his first week in Edinburgh Hector Clark went to visit the
Hoggs to introduce himself, get acquainted with the family and assure
them that both he and his team were single-minded in their determination to hunt down the killer of their daughter. Thereafter Hector Clark
never lost his feelings of compassion for the families of the victims, a sen-
timent that was shared by other policemen involved in the inquiry. That
this concern was appreciated by all those with whom they had personal
dealings was amply demonstrated at the conclusion of Robert Black's
trial in 1994. The gratitude of families who had suffered and grieved the
most more than compensated for the criticism of those who later sat back
in judgement with the benefit of hindsight.

One of Hector Clark's immediate tasks was to draw up workable parameters. Detectives were seeking a child sex killer about whom almost
nothing was known. There was a description that could have fitted tens
of thousands of men, and sightings of many vehicles including a white
van of which there were no other details.

The killer had struck in both England and Scotland, and had deposited
the bodies of his victims many miles away. It could therefore reasonably
be assumed that he was likely to be a long-distance lorry driver, or possibly a company representative or commercial traveller, but no suspect
was eliminated merely by virtue of his occupation.

Clark decided to have checked all men with serious sexual convictions
outside London and other distant cities. Additionally the checks could
only go back over men convicted during a limited number of years other-

wise the process would have been completely unmanageable. In any case, within the parameters decided upon the search would be a massive undertaking. There was to be criticism later, mainly born of hindsight, regarding both the boundary limits and perceived shortcomings in the investigation. Robert Black's only previous conviction, it should be remembered, was in March 1967, sixteen years earlier.

Hector Clark was irritated by ill-founded criticism made by those who did not appreciate the unprecedented difficulties faced by detectives on the inquiry. With virtually no clues to start with, hundreds of hours were to be spent interviewing potential witnesses and taking written statements, tracing vehicles sighted at different locations and following up hundreds of leads almost all of which were red herrings. It was to become the biggest and longest murder investigation in the United Kingdom; it was therefore inevitable that mistakes and omissions would occur.

Clark was more hurt than irritated by criticism from a different source. He realised that one or two of his senior colleagues were well intentioned, and may have had justification for disagreeing with some of his decisions. Even though he was in overall command, he knew that he was not infallible. He was aware also that many of them had considerable experience on murder inquiries. What he objected to was the critical views of one or two of those with whom he had worked being publicly aired in the press without the issues having first been raised with him. It is a tribute to Hector Clark's own professionalism that he refrained from responding publicly to his critics. He believed that public discussion of private police matters did nothing for the reputation of the police forces he was serving.

Another of Hector Clark's priorities was to meet the senior detectives from the various forces involved in the Maxwell and Hogg inquiries. His purpose was threefold: to introduce himself, to engender a team spirit among senior detectives who hitherto had themselves been in charge of major inquiries, and to make a clear statement of intention, laying out ground rules to be passed on to all those in their teams.

That first meeting between Hector Clark and most of those with whom he would be closely working during the coming months reads like a *Who's Who* of senior detectives. Detective Chief Superintendents Brian Cunningham and David Baker from Lothian and Borders and Leicestershire, Detective Superintendent Derek Boden from Staffordshire and Assistant Chief Constable Hector Clark himself, together with Detective Inspectors Les Orange and Fred Stephenson from Northumbria, were a small selection of the men who were to co-operate in the hunt for the elusive child killer.

Surveying the situation regarding both inquiries as it stood at the end of July 1983, Hector Clark was satisfied that all conventional investigative methods had been implemented, including house-to-house inquiries, vehicle checks, radio and television appeals, and hundreds of statements obtained from those whose contribution might not be of immediate use, but could be valuable when later studied in conjunction with other statements or information. Checks on known sex offenders and paedophiles had been carried out, often by officers from forces not involved with the inquiry, who on occasions interviewed suspects in the prison establishments in which they were currently incarcerated. Obtaining the written statements alone was a massive undertaking involving dozens of police officers and taking up hundreds of man-hours.

In Leicestershire, where Caroline Hogg's body had been recovered, and the lead force in that inquiry, house-to-house inquiries within a 5-mile radius of Twycross had been completed; also road blocks near the lay-by where Caroline's body had lain had been lifted after 7000 drivers had been stopped and questioned. The latest Leicestershire initiative had been to circulate to motorway service areas nationwide and other outlets, posters showing a picture of Caroline and details of her abduction and murder, with an appeal for anyone with information to contact the police.

The Hogg inquiry was in many ways a repeat of that of Susan Maxwell. In the latter case, although inquiries were still being made and leads followed up, the overall lack of progress had resulted in the investigation being gradually scaled down. With the abduction of Caroline Hogg and the subsequent discovery of her body in circumstances similar to those of Susan Maxwell, together with the linking of the two inquiries and the appointment of Hector Clark, the entire investigation had been given a fillip. It was imperative that the man they were seeking was caught before he struck again. The detectives knew that they needed a break, be it through a statement, an informant coming forward or the emergence of some vital piece of information. What they did not know was that another seven years were to elapse before that break occurred.

Another of Hector Clark's priorities upon assuming responsibility for the Maxwell and Hogg inquiries was to introduce computerised technology, the advantages of which were rapidly becoming recognised by police forces throughout the United Kingdom. The Susan Maxwell inquiry had been recorded entirely on a manual card index system. Although well tried and tested, such a method had many shortcomings. It was at best a lengthy and tedious procedure, relying for its effectiveness upon the methodical and accurate compilation, indexing and cross-referencing of thousands of cards; above all the procedure was time-consuming. The possibility of error was also too great; cards could be wrongly indexed, mislaid or even lost entirely, with the attendant risk of a vital piece of information being overlooked or, if there was an undue delay, its significance not being recognised.

Clark was painfully aware of the deficiencies that had plagued the hunt during the 1970s for Peter Sutcliffe, the Yorkshire Ripper, an inquiry in which both he and Northumbria Police had been peripherally involved. Chief among the problems encountered by the West Yorkshire murder squad had been that of recording the mass of information that had come into its possession. Police computerisation was in its infancy, and the detectives had relied upon a card index system.

The only computer available during the early part of the Black investigation was one that had recently been purchased by Lothian and Borders Police. As was to be expected, its priority was to promote efficiency within that force by storing information. At Hector Clark's prompting, space was found on its system for the Caroline Hogg inquiry, using a software program devised and written by the Lothian and Borders force's own experts. The investigating officers therefore had a computer aide for the Hogg inquiry, while still having to rely upon the card index system in the case of Susan Maxwell. This was based in Staffordshire, being the lead force in the Maxwell inquiry, and entailed the cross-checking of information by telephone with Edinburgh, a time-consuming procedure.

Reports were already coming in of a white van seen in suspicious circumstances at Sibson, only a couple of miles along the A444 from Twycross, the week before Caroline Hogg had been found.

Although Hector Clark was in overall command, both the Maxwell and Hogg investigations were carried out by those police forces within whose area either the abductions had taken place or the bodies had later been found; Northumbria and Staffordshire in the case of Susan Maxwell; Lothian and Borders and Leicestershire in that of Caroline Hogg.

The renewed surge of public interest following the discovery of Caroline Hogg's body had given fresh impetus to both murder inquiries.

Additional information flowed into the Lothian and Borders and Leicestershire murder headquarters which in Leicestershire was situated at Twycross until the end of July 1983, when it moved to the Force Communications HQ at Narborough. This facilitated the computer link-up with the other police forces involved in the investigation, and coincided with further appeals for anyone to contact them who during the past few weeks may have stopped in the lay-by where Caroline's body had been found.

Meanwhile in Portobello there emerged a witness who was convinced that he had seen Caroline in the company of a man in the Fun City amusement park. So suspicious was the witness at the time that he had written down the German registration mark of the Audi coupé in which the suspect had driven off. Scottish police immediately contacted their West German counterparts who telephoned the owner of the Audi, a forty-year-old teacher living in Witten near Dortmund. Fritz Witte had been on a motoring holiday and had been spotted while spending two nights at a Portobello guest house.

After hearing from the police, but before being questioned, Herr Witte indignantly stated publicly, 'I am not the murderer. The police think I possibly could have been, but I am not that man.' He had then gone voluntarily to the police station to be questioned, announcing afterwards, 'I went to the German police here in Witten yesterday after they telephoned me.' At the station Herr Witte had been interviewed by Detective Chief Inspector John Henry who had flown over from Edinburgh to Düsseldorf accompanied by a German-speaking interpreter.

Although four police forces were central to the Maxwell/Hogg investigation, inquiries extended throughout the United Kingdom and there was not a force which was not asked to make some inquiry regarding an individual or vehicle. Some were straightforward movement or sighting checks, others involved more detailed questioning of men with previous convictions for serious offences of a similar nature. Dozens of known killers, rapists and child molesters who roughly fitted the description of the scruffy man seen with Caroline Hogg were interrogated by detectives as far afield as Devon, Cornwall and Inverness. Although those seen were eventually eliminated from the murder inquiry, many lesser offences came to light and were often admitted, a frequent by-product of any major inquiry. Suspects in serious cases will frequently alibi themselves by admitting to minor offences elsewhere. Regional Criminal Intelligence Officers and more localised collators trawled through their retrieval systems and indexes to extract any information that could be of help to the inquiry.

Apart from arrests for minor offences, the combined effort following Hector Clark's appointment resulted in eight or nine men with paedophiliac tendencies being identified as having been in Portobello on the night of Caroline Hogg's abduction. Establishing that these child molesters had been in Portobello indicated that such men were in the habit of travelling to the resort from other parts of Scotland, a fact which 'shocked and surprised' Detective Superintendent Charles Nunn, the Lothian and Borders officer responsible for co-ordinating the Caroline Hogg inquiry. 'I honestly did not know this was happening, but men are coming from the west of Scotland, from Perthshire and from Fife . . .' he told reporters. Unfortunately none of them proved to be the man that police were seeking.

In addition there were twenty-seven witnesses who had positively identified Caroline in Portobello on the evening she disappeared, several of whom had seen her in the company of an unkempt man. Typical of these was a young lad who told police that he had seen a scruffy man, wearing tinted glasses which were pushed up into his hair and carrying a white plastic carrier bag, in Portobello on the day Caroline had disappeared. It was decided to issue to the press a police artist's drawings of the suspect compiled from witnesses' descriptions. These pictures appeared on Friday, 5 August. The response exceeded all expectations; by the following Monday the police and the newspapers had received over 500 telephone calls giving information from all parts of Britain.

An Asian family who telephoned to say that they had witnessed the abduction were quickly seen and interviewed, but their sighting proved to be mistaken. Similarly a woman from Hartlepool reported seeing a purple Marina motor car at the Bolton roundabout on the A19 in Cleveland between 6.30 p.m. and 7.0 p.m. 30 July 1982. She said that a girl resembling Susan Maxwell had been sitting in the front passenger seat. The woman agreed to be hypnotised and in her hypnotic state gave additional details, enough for Detective Chief Superintendent Brian Cunningham to announce that police were making further inquiries. It seemed that police, in their desperation, were prepared to try anything.

What was Robert Black doing during all this activity? There is every reason to believe that he was keeping up his façade of normality: going to the pub, playing darts and maintaining his close relationship with the Raysons. Despite this, many of his workmates still regarded him as a loner and a bit of an oddball. Black was a man who constantly fantasised about small girls; his urgings may have receded temporarily following the abduction of Caroline Hogg, but they were still lurking within him, ready to erupt with a renewed demand should a suitable opportunity present itself. Meanwhile there were the videos and magazines with which he could relax in the privacy of his room.

The inquiries continued during the summer and autumn of 1983, detectives experiencing highs and lows throughout that period. Michael Flynn, an Edinburgh man, raised everyone's hopes when he contacted police and told them that he and his wife had been driving north along the A697 on the evening Caroline Hogg disappeared, when at about 9.30 p.m., soon after having crossed the border into Scotland, they were nearly involved in an accident with a blue Ford Cortina which had been heading in the opposite direction. They had contacted police upon hearing of Caroline's disappearance and had provided a description of the Cortina driver which had loosely resembled Robert Black. More significantly Flynn added that accompanying the Cortina driver had been a little girl bearing a close resemblance to Caroline Hogg.

The Michael Flynn sighting had been an encouraging early lead. Everything appeared to fit into place; the time that had elapsed between Caroline Hogg's abduction and the sighting: the description of the driver and more crucially that of his young passenger. It was the job of tracing that Cortina driver that was to prove insurmountable. After early media appeals for him to come forward had failed to elicit a response, police were faced with the impossible task of tracing the driver from among 120,000 such vehicles registered with the DVLC at Swansea. Eventually well over 20,000 keepers of such vehicles were seen, interviewed and checked against known sex offenders owning such cars. Despite the huge amount of time and effort devoted to tracing the driver of the blue Cortina, which continued well into 1986, he was never found.

On Friday, 12 August 1983, Marion Beck, the four-year-old daughter of a policeman, took the part of Caroline Hogg in a reconstruction of her last outing. The re-enactment attracted hundreds of sightseers whose presence failed to impress Hector Clark: 'There were a lot of people down here who were not really interested in what was going on from our point of view, but to see what was really a macabre situation. That disappointed me.' Nothing useful resulted from the re-enactment.

Clark remained optimistic; following a headline in the *Edinburgh Evening News* of 7 September 1983 – CAROLINE: POLICE CLOSING IN – he announced later at a news conference, 'Our inquiries are at such a peak that I feel entitled to say we are getting close to him now . . .'

Detectives investigating the Susan Maxwell/Caroline Hogg abductions may have felt that they were near a breakthrough, but the reality of the situation was that, despite the massive police operation (in October, five months after her abduction, there were still 130 policemen and women employed solely on the Caroline Hogg inquiry), the combined efforts of four police forces were no nearer establishing the identity of the perpetrator.

The immense cost involved was also beginning to cause concern. At a lecture given by Hector Clark to the Lothian and Borders Police Board, the Board Chairman, Councillor Gordon Reid, took the opportunity to point out that, 'The cost was not grudged in any way, but would clearly have an effect on the Board's budget.' It was an aspect of the investigation that Clark and his senior colleagues would have to keep in mind.

The police were certainly not lacking in innovative ideas. Holiday-makers who had been in Portobello at the time of Caroline Hogg's disappearance responded to an appeal to send in any photographs or video recordings taken on the day of the abduction. They arrived from all over the world and from an indistinct image on a single snapshot a suspect who had served a seven-year prison sentence, and who fitted the description of the scruffy man seen with Caroline, was eventually traced. However, after intensive questioning the man was cleared of any involvement in the little girl's disappearance. It was another example of police effort and perseverance in tracing a suspect ending in frustration.

On Tuesday, 17 January 1984, over 250 people who were in Portobello on the evening Caroline Hogg vanished attended a meeting at the Lothian and Borders Police headquarters in Edinburgh. There they were shown a filmed reconstruction of the victim's movements on the evening of Friday, 8 July 1983, following which Detective Chief Superintendent Brian Cunningham updated them on the current state of the inquiry. The audience were then divided into discussion groups each with a senior police officer to lead them in which suggestions were made, ideas discussed and it was hoped people's memories would be jogged. The press were at the meeting and found Hector Clark to be less optimistic than he had been when speaking to them four months earlier. 'As each day passes this inquiry becomes more difficult . . .' he said.

On Saturday, 31 March 1984, the inquest into the death of Caroline Hogg, which had earlier been adjourned, was reopened at Market

Bosworth before Phillip Tomlinson, the coroner of North Leicestershire. Details of the 'massive and detailed inquiries' that police had carried out since Caroline's disappearance were given by Detective Chief Superintendent David Baker, the head of Leicestershire CID. After Dr Victor Pugh, the pathologist, had stated that death had occurred nearer 8 July 1983 (the day she was abducted) than the 18th (the day on which her body was found), an open verdict was returned. After the inquest DCS Baker told assembled reporters that police still feared a repeat killing.

The same month DCS Brian Cunningham told *The Scotsman*, 'Any inquiry that is not successful is frustrating, but this inquiry has never been at the stage where morale has been low. It is marvellous . . .' The ebullience of Cunningham's remarks to the newspaper contrasted with the sober tone of a recorded interview he had later with John Hogg, Caroline's stepfather. When commenting on the abductions of his stepdaughter and of Susan Maxwell, Hogg pointed out sadly that they were 'just two youngsters who never did anyone any harm; two young girls full of life, they had everything to live for and have just been spirited away . . . this man has proved he can move about as free as a bird and go from one place to another. I don't know, it's too much for anybody to bear.' The stepfather's grief was still weighing heavily on his mind.

The investigation continued with no let-up through the spring and into the summer of 1984. Detective Chief Inspector Stuart Henderson added his voice to that of his chief, Brian Cunningham, when he announced, 'There is no way this inquiry will be allowed to slide . . . We are all determined, no matter what, or how long it may take, to get the man responsible.'

But were determination and dedication to the task of finding the double child killer to be enough? By July 1984, two years had elapsed since Susan Maxwell's abduction and murder, and it had been a year since Caroline Hogg had suffered the same fate. Hector Clark had recently announced that the inquiry was continuing and that three new hot lines had been set up. Over 18,500 statements had been taken and 65,000 names, together with 46,000 vehicles, were listed on the police computer. Despite this the killer was still free, perhaps, as many feared, to strike again.

On Friday, 23 November 1984, following a BBC television programme the previous evening, the mother of a four-year-old boy was one of over 200 people who later got in touch with the police. She reported that a few days before Caroline's abduction, her son had what she considered to have been a lucky escape from what could have been a similar fate when a man had attempted to snatch him. He had apparently been thwarted by an unknown woman who had intervened and rescued the boy. This was another report that was taken very seriously by detectives who appealed unsuccessfully for the unknown rescuer to come forward.

The Maxwell/Hogg inquiry certainly dispelled any conception the general public may have had of stolid detectives plodding through tried and tested routines that for many years had been pursued by their predecessors. There was still a place for such methods, which had frequently proved successful in the past, but in the Robert Black inquiry more imaginative suggestions were constantly being considered by Hector Clark and his colleagues. No matter how fanciful the idea, none was immediately cast aside. Instead several were tried out in the outside hope that they might lead to the sought-for breakthrough.

In early July 1984, police attended a convention of Jehovah's Witnesses at Murreyfield Stadium in Edinburgh to appeal for anyone in the audience to contact them if they had any information they could recall from the same period the previous year at the time of Caroline Hogg's abduction.

A bizarre experiment was carried out involving the witness Flynn, who had earlier reported having narrowly avoided becoming involved in an accident with a blue Ford Cortina on the night of Caroline Hogg's abduction. He agreed to be hypnotised by a police surgeon in the hope that he would be able to recall more details of the Cortina and its occupants. Unfortunately the experiment failed, hypnosis failing to enhance the subject's recollection.

Another suspect for the Susan Maxwell murder was a travelling salesman who was interviewed in late 1985. This was a man with a history of indecency with children, who had also coincidentally sold a fire extinguisher a few weeks earlier to Fordyce Maxwell at Cramond Hill farm. The suspect was questioned by Staffordshire detectives in Northumberland before the matter was eventually submitted to the Director of Public Prosecutions who decided against taking the matter any further.

Throughout this time Robert Black was continuing his predatory ways. He admitted years later that, towards the end of 1985, three small girls had been fortunate to get away from him unharmed. In one incident near Carlisle he had enticed two girls into the front of his van on the pretext of asking for directions; fortunately for them he had selected a spot from where they could be easily seen by passers-by, so discretion for once overcame his urges, and the two girls were allowed to leave his van unharmed. At the other end of the country in South London, a ten-year-old girl ran away screaming at his approach, causing him to drive rapidly away.

By now, despite their best efforts, the lack of progress compelled police again to scale down their inquiries. It was decided at a meeting between Hector Clark (who by this time had been appointed Deputy Chief Constable of Lothian and Borders Police) and senior officers from the other forces that the investigation should be wound down. It was a shattering blow to the morale of all those who for so long had devoted themselves to the murder hunt, but it was considered that the expenditure of manpower and resources that had been required to sustain the investigation for almost two and a half years was no longer justified in view of the results so far achieved. The Staffordshire and Edinburgh incident rooms were closed down, although occasional reports on suspicious incidents of a similar nature in England and Scotland continued to be closely looked at. Otherwise the inquiry lay dormant.

In March 1986, news of Sarah Harper's abduction over 150 miles away in Morley near Leeds, and of the recovery of her body from the River Trent close to Nottingham, was greeted by Hector Clark with some caution. In concurrence with other senior colleagues, and after studying the circumstances of the latest abduction, they agreed that the similarities with the abductions of Susan Maxwell and Caroline Hogg were too few to justify immediate linking. Clark kept an open mind on the possibility that the Harper case could be the work of the same man, but was content for the time being to leave Detective Chief Superintendent Tom Newton and Detective Superintendent John Stainthorpe to carry on with the latest inquiry, while monitoring its progress. It was agreed that there should be a computer link between the incident room at Holbeck in West Yorkshire, and the one in Edinburgh, and a telephone hot line between West Yorkshire and Staffordshire.

Meanwhile police were still trying to trace a light blue car, a Morris Marina and a Triumph 2000 seen in or near Coldstream on the day Susan Maxwell disappeared. The following month, in a tone of despondency, Hector Clark told *The Scotsman*, 'Without more information from the public, we can go no further in our investigation.' He went on to say that police were still seeking to interview a man seen with a little girl resembling Caroline Hogg in Bath Street, Portobello, walking towards the High Street at around 7.30 p.m. on the evening she vanished.

Just before Christmas 1986, following a suggestion by John Brownlow, one of Her Majesty's Inspectors of Constabulary, there was formed a single database for the three child murder inquiries. The new facility was sited at Tyrls police station in Bradford which was already connected up to HOLMES (Home Office Large Major Enquiry System). Information had recently come to light that strongly indicated a connection between the three crimes. This decision was therefore a logical progression, and was not intended to be a criticism of the one made earlier.

It was a formidable undertaking to back-record all the information on to a single database. Over forty part-time typists, backed up by specialist police officers, were employed on this task which, when completed, enabled the information gathered in from the three inquiries to be immediately accessible to all officers engaged on those inquiries. By January 1987, detectives knew that they were hunting for a serial child killer, and the Bradford incident room, now known as the Child Murder Bureau, was manned by personnel from four police forces.

Soon after the setting up of the Child Murder Bureau, Hector Clark agreed to include the Harper inquiry with that of Maxwell and Hogg. Clark was indeed now 'El Supremo', having the West Yorkshire and Nottinghamshire forces also under his wing. The inquiries being computer-linked facilitated the speedy and accurate dissemination of information that was common to all three. For Lothian and Borders Police, being linked to the HOLMES system eased some of the workload their system had previously handled.

The decision to include the Sarah Harper inquiry with that of Susan Maxwell and Caroline Hogg gave added impetus and a new perspective to the work already being carried out by the West Yorkshire detectives headed by Tom Newton and John Stainthorpe. Together with detectives from the other forces, they were constantly reviewing progress and thinking up new initiatives after their daily sifting through of the Bradford database to seek out likely suspects and to introduce new lines of inquiry.

Nearly a year had passed since Sarah Harper's abduction and detectives were no closer to nailing the killer who they were satisfied was responsible for the three murders. By this time each force had access to HOLMES, the sophisticated database which eliminated much of the tedious routine work that had plagued the early stages of the inquiries. They were now fully co-ordinated under one man, but each force retained its autonomy.

The Child Murder Bureau at Bradford had been set up with authority to try out new inventive investigative methods and techniques in the hope of obtaining a breakthrough. A reasearch unit, consisting of officers from the six forces, trawled through the database and studied suggested avenues of approach. It was the first occasion in the history of British policing that there has been such a technically sophisticated murder inquiry, involving hundreds of men and women from the uniformed and detective branches.

In March 1987, on the first anniversary of Sarah Harper's disappearance, Detective Superintendent John Stainthorpe made another emotional appeal: 'I am sure someone is covering up for the killer. If they are doing it because they love him, I can only say that a person like that is not worth loving,' he announced starkly.

Two months later hopes were raised briefly when Northumbria Police questioned a former travelling salesman in connection with the Harper murder. He was one of many people that were questioned, but for several reasons his interrogation gave rise to more than usual optimism. However, this confidence evaporated when the suspect was able to prove that he had been detained under the Mental Health Act between October 1985 and April 1987.

So the investigation continued; leads were followed up as information regularly filtered into the Bradford nerve centre. Prospective witnesses were interviewed, informants were cultivated and the occasional suspect was hauled in for questioning. Hector Clark and his senior colleagues were always receptive to ideas, suggestions and information from wheresoever they came. No one knew when, where or from whom would come the vital piece of information that would re-energise the inquiry and lead to the triple killer. Nothing emerged.

Details of an incident which took place in April 1988 in Nottingham, when a fifteen-year-old girl only escaped being abducted by virtue of her own courage and the timely intervention of her boyfriend, were never passed to detectives investigating the three child murders and abductions. Had the information been sent on, including a description of the attacker and his van, it would certainly have given impetus to the Scottish and Midland inquiries, and may even have brought closer Robert Black's arrest. Instead, three months later Hector Clark pessimistically announced, 'We have to admit that we are not now making real progress, but I am convinced that someone in this country still has suspicions . . . I urge them to come forward now, even at this late stage, to help us.'

It was a bitter pill to have to swallow, not only for the detectives who had been pursuing the investigation for six years, but for the victims' families. There was a brief flurry of activity a week later when a report of four attempted child abductions in the West Midlands by a man and woman in a car was investigated, but it soon became apparent that there was no connection with the main inquiry. It was therefore left to the local police to follow up.

The families of the three girl victims had to reconcile themselves to the likelihood that the man responsible for the death of their children would escape retribution. With this knowledge, the families still had to try and rebuild their lives. In 1989, three years after her daughter had been killed, Jackie Harper exhibited her own brand of stoicism when she told a reporter from the *Derby Evening Telegraph*: 'You are either going to go under, or you are going to turn round and fight back. But obviously if you do that you are going to become a bit harder . . . You have to be careful that you don't carry a chip on your shoulder. I have just picked myself up and got on with my life.'

At the end of January 1990, detectives from Lothian and Borders reinterviewed suspects from the Derby area. To explain this renewal of interest a police spokesman said at the time, 'These men who are being interviewed have all been spoken to over the last few years . . . We just want to clarify a few points in their statements.'

By February 1990, the HOLMES database contained names of over 185,000 people and 57,000 statements. That effort and little to show for it had a demoralising effect upon the detectives; until, that is, the middle of July the same year when a vigilant and astute member of the public was doing a spot of weekend gardening . . .

CHAPTER 8

A TWO-MINUTE WALK

It was a desolate evening in Morley, south of Leeds. Rain was beating down and gusts of a bitter north-easterly wind discouraged most people from venturing far away from their hearths and television programmes. In a small, back-to-back end-of-terrace house in Brunswick Place, an unmade cul-de-sac surrounded by a maze of other small streets, twenty-six-year-old Jackie Harper, a divorced mother of three children, was finishing her tea. With her were Sarah (ten), Claire (nine) and David (five).

It was twenty minutes to eight on the evening of Wednesday, 26 March 1986, when Mrs Harper asked Sarah to run along to the corner shop in Peel Street, less than 200 yards away, to buy a loaf of bread and two packets of crisps. Fair-haired Sarah, a junior cornet-playing member of the local Salvation Army band, didn't hesitate. She asked Claire if she wanted to accompany her, but her sister declined as she was still finishing her tea, so donning her anorak Sarah prepared to go alone.

She left No. 1 Brunswick Place and turned left, the hood of her anorak pulled up and with an empty lemonade bottle clasped in each hand intending to claim back the 'return on empties'. A third of the way along Brunswick Place was the first of two snickets, alleyways leading between the houses into Peel Street which ran parallel. Sarah passed through one of them before turning right to continue along Peel Street towards the shop.

She entered K & M Stores and found the owner's wife, Hiralel Champaneri, chatting to Mrs Jackson from the fish and chip shop opposite. The Champaneris had recently acquired the shop and were open long hours to serve the small local community. No one paid any attention to the fat, bald-headed man who followed Sarah into the shop and left just before she did without buying anything. After paying Bina, the Champaneris' thirteen-year-old daughter, for her bread and packets of crisps, Sarah left the shop and turned towards home. Two of her friends from Middle Street Junior School, Nicola Gregson and Joanne Mitchell, saw her from a distance in Peel Street seconds before she turned into one of the snickets leading back into Brunswick Place. It was the last time Sarah Harper was seen alive.

Jackie Harper could not understand why Sarah had not returned from her errand. It should have taken her no more than ten minutes to get to the shop and back, yet it was now half-past eight and there was no sign of her. She opened the front door and scanned the street, but nobody was about. She told Claire to go and look for her sister and to tell her to hurry up, but minutes later the little girl returned and told her mother that she had been unable to find her sister. Alarmed, Jackie hurriedly put on her anorak and, leaving Claire in charge of David, hastened along Brunswick Place and Peel Street to K & M Stores. Sarah had left there some time ago, Bina Champaneri told her. Jackie left the shop and ran back home; still Sarah had not returned. By now it was almost 9 p.m. and over an hour had passed since her daughter had left on her errand. There was only one thing left for the frantic woman to do: notify the police that Sarah was missing.

Although Hector Clark was informed of Sarah Harper's disappearance, and the subsequent recovery of her body from the River Trent near Nottingham, several months were to elapse before her abduction and murder were linked directly to those of Susan Maxwell and Caroline Hogg. There were valid reasons for this interruption in the investigative continuity of the inquiry.

Foremost were the differing circumstances surrounding Sarah Harper's abduction and that of the other two girls. Sarah had been snatched on a bleak, wet evening in March. Wearing a dark-coloured anorak with the hood almost entirely hiding her face, she could be scarcely recognised as a young girl, whereas there could have been no mistaking the appeal and attractiveness of the other two victims. Each was taken in broad daylight on a hot Friday in July, and both were dressed appropriately in summer clothes.

Then there were the contrasting locations from which the girls had been snatched: Susan Maxwell from rural Northumberland close to the Scottish border, Caroline Hogg from a busy seaside resort east of Edinburgh, while Sarah Harper had disappeared from an urban backwater more than 150 miles away in West Yorkshire.

Another possible consideration, although one never publicly voiced, may have been the cost involved of reactivating the dormant Maxwell/Hogg inquiries without first having very good reason to suspect that all three girls had fallen victim to the same killer. Together this resulted in there being no link made between the cases until November 1986. In the meantime the latest inquiry would be headed by Detective Chief Superintendent Tom Newton, and Detective Superintendent John Stainthorpe, head of Leeds South Division of the West Yorkshire Police, which included Morley.

An immediate search was set in hand from the police station in Corporation Street following the distraught call from Jackie Harper. It continued through the night but by the morning no sign of the missing girl had been found. Early the next day a house-to-house inquiry was commenced in the vicinity of Brunswick Place and Peel Street, while the search was concentrated on an area near Morley town centre bounded by Clough Street, Middleton Road, Albert Road and Queen Street. Dozens of uniformed policemen and women, including dog handlers, searched likely places of concealment and child hideaways. The dogs sniffed their way through Lewisham Park near the Harpers' home, while British Transport police officers searched in and around Morley railway station and the adjacent lines. At nearby Tingley underwater units trawled the reservoir.

The concern felt by police over the ten-year-old's disappearance was voiced at a later press conference by John Stainthorpe: 'As far as I can tell there is no reason why this girl should go missing. While I am keeping an open mind, obviously I am treating it very seriously . . . We cannot discount the possibility that she has been abducted.'

Back at the Harpers' home at 1 Brunswick Place, the family were rallying round a heavily sedated Jackie Harper. Terry, her ex-husband and father of Sarah, arrived from his home in Ingle Avenue, Morley; her mother Marlene Hopton was there together with Jackie's stepfather Dennis, while a member of the Salvation Army called to give comfort.

The search for Sarah Harper followed a predictable course. On Friday, 28 March, two days after her disappearance, 200 local people, some with a citizen's band radio link-up, responded to a police loudspeaker appeal and arrived at Newlands Junior School not far from the Harpers' home, to assist over 100 policemen and women already engaged on the search. They were divided into teams of about fifteen, each led by a police officer; while some concentrated their search on open spaces and waste land, others converged on the more built-up areas within a one-mile radius of Brunswick Place.

John Hope was one of the volunteers who took part: 'You see these searches carried out on the news, but never really think you will be involved in one. During the search for Sarah Harper I discovered parts of Morley and the surrounding neighbourhood that I never knew existed, and I've lived here most of my life. It shows how thorough the search was.'

Meanwhile, during extended house-to-house inquiries, police officers made their first visit to the premises of Myles and Spencer which were situated only 200 yards from the spot where it was believed Sarah was abducted. It was later established that Black had called on the company early on the evening of 26 March and delivered some posters, a fact which unfortunately did not emerge when police visited. It was a lapse that in the long run arguably prolonged the time taken in tracing Robert Black.

Even this early in the inquiry, by Saturday with no trace of the missing girl having been found locally, police were considering the possibility that she had been taken away from the Morley area. Nevertheless John Stainthorpe was still hopeful: 'I am still optimistic she may be found safe and well, but bearing in mind the abduction aspect, her description has now been circulated nationwide,' he told reporters. Later a telex was sent out to all forces requesting that a search be carried out in areas where previous child victims had been found. A police incident room had been set up at Holbeck police station, Detective Superintendent Stainthorpe's headquarters; from there West Yorkshire Police co-ordinated what by this time was a nationwide inquiry.

Meanwhile local inquiries continued. A mobile police station was sited at the end of Peel Street near the junction with Johnson Street. Posters depicting Sarah and giving details of her disappearance were displayed in the windows, and members of the public called in regularly with snippets of information.

With still no news of her missing daughter, the suffering of Jackie Harper, her family and her estranged husband Terry continued. Jackie, still under sedation, was prohibited by her doctor from speaking to the press. It was Marlene Hopton who announced that her daughter had become resigned to Sarah's death. 'I believe she's dead, and Jackie believes so,' she told reporters.

Jackie's ex-husband was equally distraught. Terry Harper joined the early searches for his daughter, but by the following week he seemed to be near despair. He told the *Yorkshire Evening Post*, 'I don't know how long I can hang on or how much more I can take . . . The worry is killing me. It's just not knowing one way or the other.' Police had visited Terry late on the night of his daughter's disappearance to check on whether she was with him; if not, to ask him if he had any idea as to her whereabouts. Six days later he was visited again by a squad of detectives who searched the flat he shared with his girlfriend at Rothwell near Leeds. Although finding it to be an unnerving experience, he accepted the police intrusion equably. 'It is their job, I know that,' he told a reporter.

A few days after Sarah's disappearance, a pre-arranged talk to local children given by Stuart Pearson, the local community policeman, at the Morley Salvation Army hall, took on an added sense of relevance in view of the recent events. Around this time also a local man called George Bailey went into the mobile police station in Peel Street and told an interesting story. He said that on the evening Sarah had gone missing he had been in K & M Stores at the same time as the little girl. He had noticed a stranger lingering in the shop but had thought nothing about it until the previous evening when he said he had seen the same man driving an old green Saab motor car in Morley.

For nearly a week police had been mounting nightly road checks on all roads leading into the area surrounding Brunswick Place and Peel Street. Every vehicle entering or leaving had been stopped, its driver questioned and particulars of the vehicle recorded. It was thus a simple matter to check on whether a green Saab had been seen during that period. There was no record of such a vehicle having been stopped, but it was possible that the car had slipped through the net. A check was therefore made of all green Saabs registered in the United Kingdom. It was a huge undertaking but at the end of it police were satisfied that no car fitting that description had been in Morley during the evening of 26 March. Bailey had either misidentified the make of the car or its driver. Police erroneously concluded that, having made a mistake about the car, he could have been equally wrong about the man he said he had seen in K & M Stores. It was only after Robert Black's arrest that it was seen how like him had been the police artist's impression drawn from Bailey's description.

Despite such setbacks detectives continued to follow up other leads. On Thursday, 3 April, police appealed for a young man in his twenties to come forward who had been spotted on the evening of Sarah Harper's disappearance eight days before in a snicket leading from Brunswick Place into Peel Street. The following day a young man came forward and satisfied police that he had been in Morley to meet a friend. He was eliminated from the inquiry.

Several people had mentioned seeing a bearded man in Peel Street earlier, and a woman out walking her dog in the rain at about 7.30 p.m. remembered a man with a beard getting into a van parked adjacent to Brunswick Place.

Two familiar exercises were carried out on the Thursday. A little girl resembling Sarah Harper was dressed in similar clothes to those worn by her on the night she went missing; she then retraced the missing girl's route to and from her home to K & M Stores. As with Caroline Hogg, the reconstruction produced no tangible result. In the evening Jackie Harper made a tearful appeal on television, begging for news of her daughter: 'I just want her back, even if she's dead. If someone would just pick up the phone and tell us where the body is . . .' she pleaded.

In a community such as Morley where most people knew each other, the impact of Sarah Harper's disappearance was especially traumatic. Almost everyone had known the little girl who had attended the local junior school, and who was regularly seen playing with her friends in the neighbourhood. Several local people felt themselves to be under suspicion following routine police questioning. Richard Simpson, a thirty-four-year-old ceiling fixer, told a *Yorkshire Evening Post* reporter that when detectives interviewed him he had found it hard at first to recall where he had been on the Wednesday evening. He then remembered that he had been out having a drink with a friend, later returning home to find police swamping the area.

Mrs Lynne Owen, a mother of three who was a neighbour of the Harpers in Brunswick Place, said that since being stopped and spoken to by the police she had 'found myself looking at everyone, wondering whether they had done anything to the girl'.

During the week following Sarah's disappearance, Colin Sampson, the Chief Constable of West Yorkshire Police, sought to reassure people that there would be no let-up in police efforts to discover what had happened to the missing girl. At a meeting of the West Yorkshire Police Authority on 9 April, he outlined the police inquiry to date and told them, 'The search for her will continue unabated until some result, whatever it may be, is achieved.'

Although almost three years had elapsed since Caroline Hogg had been abducted, already some newspapers were suggesting that the latest disappearance may have been linked to that of Hogg. At this stage John Stainthorpe did not consider it likely, the circumstances of Sarah's disappearance being in many respects unlike that of the Scottish girl. Hector Clark also thought the dissimilarities were too many and varied to suggest that the disappearances of Susan Maxwell, Caroline Hogg and Sarah Harper were the work of one man. Nevertheless neither detective discounted entirely the possibility that the killer of Maxwell and Hogg had struck again.

By Wednesday, 9 April 1986, with the missing girl inquiry now into its fourteenth day, police were giving up hope of finding Sarah Harper alive. John Stainthorpe appealed at a press conference to relatives or friends of anyone whom they might suspect for any reason of involvement in Sarah Harper's disappearance to contact police. At the same time he voiced police fears: 'We must accept that she may well now be dead, but there is still a very slim chance she is still alive and we will continue searching until we find either her or her body.' The appeal coincided with the nationwide distribution of a poster showing a picture of the missing girl and asking that anyone with information about her contact the police.

On the day Peel Street Junior School reassembled after the Easter holiday, the headmaster Mr Reuben Robson led the children in prayer for their missing schoolfriend. It was a sad assembly with many of Sarah's friends close to tears. The sombre mood at the school reflected the feeling that still pervaded Morley and the surrounding area. George Jackson, a regular at the Miner's Arms, recalled that 'for weeks everyone felt under a cloud. The women especially were worried about their kids. They used to take them to school and then pick them up in the afternoon. Before the girl went missing most of them would go to school on their own.'

A mother remembered that any stranger seen about Morley immediately aroused suspicion. 'I'm sure there must have been lots of reps and others calling at the factories who wondered why everyone was giving them funny looks.'

West Yorkshire Police already had one major technological advantage over the forces involved in the Maxwell and Hogg inquiries: it was joined to the computerised data management system HOLMES. This is best described as a computerised card index containing millions of individual convictions, capable of retrieving vital information about suspects relating to their *modus operandi*, clothes, personal description and other details. Although able to retrieve a vast amount of information relating to known sex offenders, there was no reason at this stage for it to single out Robert Black. He had no record of offending in the Midlands, and his only sexual conviction had been in 1963 at Greenock Sheriff court. HOLMES did however facilitate the elimination of other known sex offenders who lived in, or frequented, the region.

A few days later a mystery caller telephoned the police at Barnsley professing to know the whereabouts of Sarah Harper and the identity of the person responsible for her disappearance. He promised to phone back later but failed to do so. It was another example of the many false calls and anonymous letters that plagued the inquiry team.

John Stainthorpe referred scathingly to the bogus telephone informants and letter writers as 'nutters'. He was particularly scornful about self-styled psychics who claimed to know what had happened to Sarah. A blunt, pragmatic Yorkshireman, he directed that all letters from psychics were to be immediately thrown away on the premise that the sender, having supernatural powers, would be aware that his original letter had been disposed of, and so would write again. Similarly, if detectives had occasion to call on a psychic they were instructed not to announce their identity, but to wait until the psychic had demonstrated his mystic power by identifying them as policemen. Such responses to both letters and visits no doubt led to some interesting situations.

As events transpired, such help in tracing the whereabouts of Sarah Harper was soon to be rendered unnecessary. On the morning of Saturday, 19 April 1986, seventeen days after she had vanished from a back street in Morley, thirty-seven-year-old David Moult, out walking his dog Ben along the bank of the River Trent at Wilford, near Nottingham, noticed what he thought was a piece of sacking floating in the river. The vagaries of the swiftly flowing water suddenly turned the 'sacking' over – Sarah Harper had been found . . .

Although Hector Clark and his team made no immediate connection between the latest abduction and murder and the earlier ones, Detective Chief Superintendent Tom Newton, head of the Eastern Area of the West Yorkshire CID, and Detective Superintendent John Stainthorpe had access via their computer to the mass of data that had already been accumulated by detectives investigating the Maxwell and Hogg murders.

John Stainthorpe at first shared Hector Clark's doubt about the likelihood of the Sarah Harper murder being the work of the same man who had kidnapped and killed Susan Maxwell and Caroline Hogg; after Sarah's body had been recovered from the Trent he revised his opinion. The proximity of Wilford to Loxley and Twyford where the other victims had been found seemed more than coincidental, especially when considered with other similarities to the Maxwell/Hogg cases.

Stainthorpe was careful to keep his views about the matter to himself, deliberately dissuading the media from making a premature connection between the three cases. 'There has been widespread speculation linking the murder of Sarah with other child murders,' he said. 'I would like to make it clear that there is no firm evidence to link her murder with that of other children. However, I want to stress I am keeping the options open. I still feel the murder of Sarah is connected with her home town of Morley.'

'Although by the time Sarah's body was found I suspected a link with the other inquiries, I didn't want this to become generally known,' John Stainthorpe explained. 'I was appealing at that time for anyone with suspicions of relatives or friends to come forward. If anyone had had doubts about someone in connection with Sarah Harper's murder, and I had revealed that I thought the same person could have been responsible for the other two killings, the informant may not have come forward, perhaps knowing that whoever he suspected had a cast-iron alibi for the other murders'.

Stainthorpe and the other detectives moved to Nottingham and set up a major incident room at the city's Radford Road police station, there to work closely with the Nottinghamshire Police. Two years later the same venue was to be the centre of an inquiry into a vicious assault on a young girl.

Examination of the river bank near where Sarah Harper had been found failed to determine whether she had been alive when thrown into the river; this was only confirmed at the post-mortem examination which also indicated that she had been in the water for about three weeks. A further difference between the Harper case and those of Maxwell and Hogg was that Sarah showed signs of having been seriously assaulted before being dumped in the water, while the other girls had displayed no such evidence. Finally, apart from one or two items lying nearby, Susan Maxwell had been dressed when found, whereas Caroline Hogg had been discovered naked, and several items of Sarah's clothing were missing.

A combing of the banks of the River Trent and of its tributaries the Soar and Derwent was carried out by the police of four forces (Nottinghamshire, Staffordshire, Derbyshire and Leicestershire). Hundreds of uniformed officers were supported by specialist units including dog handlers, mounted officers and teams in inflatable boats. With the help of water-flow experts from British Waterways, who were responsible for the upkeep of rivers and canals in the area, it was estimated that Sarah Harper's body had entered the water in the River Soar and that at some time during the past three weeks it had been caught up

Susan Maxwell
(News Team International Limited, Birmingham)

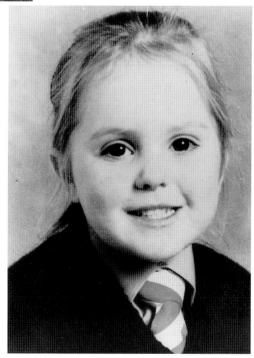

aroline Hogg
'ews Team International Limited,
rmingham)

Police poster for Sarah Harper
(West Yorkshire Police)

DID YOU SEE SARAH?

◄ SARAH JAYNE HARPER, aged 10 years, 4ft. 2in. tall, fair complexion, blonde hair (straight, collar-length). Last seen in Peel Street, Morley, near Leeds at 8.05 p.m. on Wednesday, 26th March, 1986.

At this time she was carrying a medium-sized sliced loaf of white bread in a Warburton's blue and white greaseproof wrapper and was dressed in clothing similar to that shown in these photographs: Light blue anorak (with fold-away hood), burgundy jumper, pale pink cord skirt, white knee-length socks, white flower-patterned vest, blue cotton briefs and brown shoes. ▼

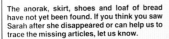

CAN YOU HELP?

The anorak, skirt, shoes and loaf of bread have not yet been found. If you think you saw Sarah after she disappeared or can help us to trace the missing articles, let us know.

If you have any information, telephone Leeds (0532) 707599/707548 or Nottingham (0602) 706060/706622, or speak to any Police Officer.

Sarah Harper
(News Team International Limited, Birmingham)

The A697 towards Cornhill. The gateway into the field on the left is where Black is believed to have reversed his van before abducting Susan Maxwell. (*Robert Church*)

Brunswick Place Morley. Sarah Harper lived at No 1. (*Robert Church*)

OFFICERS FROM ROBERT BLACK CHILD MURDERS TEAM. L TO R

Detective Chief Inspector Dennis Cleugh, Northumbria Police, Detective Superintendent (ret'd) John Stainthorpe, West Yorkshire Police, Detective Constable Tony Beardmore, Staffordshire Police, Detective Chief Inspector Stuart Henderson, Lothian and Borders Police, Detective Constable Tony Leighton, Staffordshire Police, Detective Superintendent Peter Herward, Staffordshire Police, Detective Constable Brian Luton, Staffordshire Police, Woman Detective Constable Alex Starkovitch, Staffordshire Police, Detective Inspector Peter Robinson, West Yorkshire Police, Chief Inspector Bert Shivas, Leicestershire Constabulary, Detective Constable Peter Noone, Staffordshire Police, Woman Police Constable Ann Melrose, Lothian and Borders Police, Detective Sergeant (ret'd) Don Norton, West Yorkshire Police, Detective Chief Inspector Roger Orr, Lothian and Borders Police, Assistant Chief Constable Andrew Brown, Lothian and Borders Police (succeeded Hector Clark on his retirement as officer i/c inquiry), Detective Constable Alan Cossar, Lothian and Borders Police, Detective Constable Dave Barnes, Nottinghamshire Constabulary, Detective Sergeant Gary Brothwell, Nottinghamshire Constabulary, Detective Constable Ian McClure, Lothian and Borders Police (Exhibits officer), Detective Constable Keith Seymour, Nottinghamshire Constabulary, Police Sergeant Alan Haigh, West Yorkshire Police, Detective Superintendent James Temple, Lothian and Borders Police (Deputy Senior Investigating Officer), Deputy Chief Constable Hector Clark, Lothian and Borders Police (Officer i/c Child Murder Inquiry).

by a riverside obstruction. This would have accounted for the delay in the body reaching the spot from which it was recovered.

Sarah Harper's body was found at 9.30 a.m. on Saturday, 19 April, and within three hours John Stainthorpe had arrived on the scene, together with Detective Chief Superintendent Terry Cox, the head of Nottinghamshire CID. Immediate inquiries were set in hand. Police were particularly anxious to find the missing articles of clothing and the missing loaf of Warburton's bread which Sarah had been carrying when last seen, and which was not sold in the Nottingham area. Finding any of these items, it was hoped, would give an indication as to where the girl's body had entered the water as well as the possible route taken by her killer from Morley to Nottingham. Meanwhile Terry Harper, Sarah's father, had the harrowing task of officially identifying the partly decomposed body of his daughter. 'It was worse than I ever dreamed of,' a shaken Mr Harper said later.

While her ex-husband undertook the grim mission of identifying his daughter, Jackie Harper had the equally distressing task of informing her other children of their sister's death. It proved to be equally harrowing. Nine-year-old Claire ran upstairs and ransacked the bedroom that she had shared with Sarah, while David, unable yet to comprehend the significance of recent events, tearfully told his mother that he believed that Sarah had gone to Jesus.

The increasing police concern at the growing number of child murders was evident at a summit meeting held at Scotland Yard on Monday, 21 April. Top-ranking detectives and other senior officers representing sixteen police forces were in attendance. The meeting had been convened by Commander Phillip Corbett, head of the Yard's C11 (Criminal Intelligence) Branch. Those present gave details of the current state of several child murder inquiries including the Maxwell, Hogg and Harper cases, as well as those of Genette Tate who had disappeared in Devon in 1978, Marion Crofts, a fourteen-year-old who was raped and beaten to death in Hampshire three years later, and Mark Tildesley, aged seven, who vanished on his way to a funfair at Wokingham in 1984.

Among the suggestions and information emerging at the conference was a proposal that an American psychologist be invited across from the United States to compile a profile of a sex killer. The psychological profiling technique was already an established aide in murder inquiries in the USA but in the summer of 1986 it was to be another eighteen months before John Duffy, the railway killer who raped and killed three women, was sentenced to life imprisonment at the Old Bailey following a pro-longed investigation in which David Canter, then a Professor of Psychology at Surrey University, had drawn up a remarkably accurate profile of Duffy. From that time onwards profiling was increasingly adopted in major investigations. In the case of Robert Black it was to be January 1988 before the result of a psychological profile drawn up by the FBI was announced.

Meanwhile Superintendent John Stainthorpe repeated his appeal for witnesses: 'Someone out there has an idea in their mind as to who may be responsible. I beg them, please come forward, it matters not if you are wrong, our inquiries are carried out very discreetly,' he told the *Derby Evening Telegraph*.

During these early days of the murder inquiry, suspect persons, together with witnesses and vehicles, in West Yorkshire and Nottinghamshire were checked against the Edinburgh computer database which contained details of the Hogg inquiry, and records at Staffordshire where the inquiry into the Susan Maxwell case, although run down, was still open.

On Friday, 24 April 1986, John Stainthorpe appeared on BBC's *Crimewatch*. The programme was primarily appealing for help with the Susan Maxwell and Caroline Hogg inquiries, and the item referring to the Harper case was fitted in at the last moment. In it Stainthorpe appealed for information, and drew attention in particular to Sarah Harper's shoes, anorak and skirt which had still not been recovered. After the pro-gramme dozens of people telephoned in with information, despite which detectives the next day announced that they were 'a trifle disappointed' with the outcome. The missing items of clothing and the bread were never found. Experts were nevertheless able to deduce that Sarah had almost certainly been dumped in the River Soar within twenty-four hours of being abducted.

Detectives were interested, however, in two letters received from a woman calling herself Alice in which she said that she had been in Dundee on 26 March in company with a man who had told her that the same afternoon he would be travelling to Edinburgh and then south towards the Midlands. Alice had not elaborated further, but had dis-closed enough information to intrigue police and encourage them to meet her. Such was not to be; Alice had not revealed her full name or her address, and appeals for her to come forward proved unavailing.

After the search for clues along the river bank, Nottinghamshire Police issued another appeal for fishermen, pleasure boat owners or anyone else who had been on the River Trent for whatever purpose to contact them, but again nothing useful resulted.

Two weeks after Sarah Harper's body had been found, the hunt for her killer was at its height. House-to-house searches and inquiries were going ahead, while in the West Yorkshire Police incident room at Holbeck alone a hundred police officers manned the thirteen computer terminals linked to the Nottingham incident room. The banks of several rivers had been searched, and dozens of potential witnesses seen and their statements obtained.

Superintendent John Stainthorpe: 'Any murder investigation where the victim and assailant have no connection with each other, in other words they are not known to each other, is a very arduous investigation. You have got to have a lot of luck – some people say you make your own luck, and to a degree that's true – but you can waste a lot of time.'

At the beginning of May 1986, teams of police officers descended on a number of M1 motorway service areas as far apart as Woolley Edge near Wakefield, Woodall at Sheffield and Trowell to the west of Nottingham. There they questioned motorists and other motorway users who may have been on the motorway on 26/27 March 1986, and who may have noticed something unusual or amiss. Particular attention was drawn to a white Transit van. It was a long shot, but as a police spokesman said at the time, 'It is logical to assume that the offender drove from Morley to Nottingham along the M1, bearing in mind the distance from the motorway to the spot where she [Sarah Harper] was found.'

On Saturday, 24 June yet another public appeal was made by the police, this time for the driver of a Ford Sierra to come forward. A witness had been to the police and reported that on the night of 26 March he had been driving from the M1 along the A453 towards Radcliffe on Soar when he had noticed a Ford Sierra pull off the road on to a track leading down to the river. The driver of the Sierra failed to respond to the police appeal, but as it turned out he would in any event have been eliminated from the inquiry.

Ten days later, on 1 July, the funeral of Sarah Harper took place at Morley in the Salvation Army citadel in which she had been a member of the band. It was a sad ceremony attended by the little girl's family and friends, including several of her sobbing school pals.

It was about this time that West Yorkshire Police initiated a comprehensive trawl through its records to seek out men with convictions for indecency offences. A request for a similar search to be carried out was also made to the chief officers of surrounding forces. The intelligence officers in each local division, and those further afield, were required to provide details of all men in their respective recording systems who had been convicted of:

(a)   indecent exposure,
(b)   indecent assault,
(c)   violence towards children,
(d)   abduction, or attempted abduction,
(e)   rape.

When the searches had been completed, and the results forwarded to the West Yorkshire incident room, the cases were prioritised:

(1)   The case to be carefully scrutinised and the subject closely inter-
       viewed.
(2)   Most of the cases to be investigated and the majority of the subjects
       interviewed.
(3)   Less intensive scrutiny, and fewer subjects interviewed.
(4)   Of only slight interest as it was considered that subjects falling into
       this category were unlikely to have been involved in anything as
       serious as the Sarah Harper abduction and murder.

Although the culprit did not emerge from this exercise, it could be said that had such a trawl been carried out earlier in Scotland, the result may have been different. Had attention there been focused on men with early convictions for minor sexual offences, or those dealt with leniently for relatively serious offences, Robert Black may well have emerged.

As we have seen, following Hector Clark's appointment as El Supremo one of his first actions had been to instigate a trawl. This had necessarily to be contained within manageable parameters, including the number of years it went back. It should be remembered that Robert Black's only conviction for a sexual offence had been sixteen years earlier when in 1967 he had been sentenced to Borstal training. Before then there had been only the admonishment administered in 1963 at Greenock Sheriff's court.

Arguments relating to the respective methods of trawling, and the parameters within which they were applied, are largely academic. Senior detectives in charge of the various inquiries adopted methods they considered to be the most likely to bring about a successful outcome. It so happened that neither method of searching through previous convictions drew out Robert Black.

The investigation continued through 1986. By July 200 West Yorkshire and Nottinghamshire detectives and uniformed officers were still working on the case. Other statistics were equally impressive. 15,000 people had been interviewed and over 1400 statements obtained. 10,000 leaflets had been distributed in the Morley area alone while 3000 properties had been searched, including two visits to the premises of Myles and Spencer and the adjacent builder's yards.

One of the most innovative developments during this time had been the forming of one computer database for the three murders. Henceforth inquiries would be computer-linked, thus facilitating the speedy and accurate retrieval and dissemination of information relevant to all three. Only time would tell whether this would hasten the capture of the man who so far had eluded them.

CHAPTER 9

A THWARTED ATTEMPT

Robert Black had changed to a blue Transit van with a side opening door by the time he set out on Saturday, 23 April 1988 on another weekend trip. This time his journey was to the Midlands and north-west including Birmingham, Manchester, Stoke and Nottingham. As so often before, his weekend started uneventfully. By Sunday afternoon the weather was warm and sunny as he drove towards Nottingham where he had posters to drop off at the depot of Mills and Allen.

Teresa Thornhill looked younger than her fifteen years. Just 4 ft 11 ins tall, wearing a pink blouse and skirt and white socks, she looked nearer eleven or twelve. It was past 7 p.m. when she and her boyfriend Andrew Beeston left the Forest Recreation Ground in the Forest Fields district of the city to stroll home together in the balmy spring evening.

A few minutes before, Robert Black had made his delivery at Mills and Allen on Gregory Boulevard and was now pursuing one of his favourite activities, that of cruising slowly round the neighbouring streets. He had felt the urge coming on earlier and by now was feeling an overwhelming need to relieve his repressed excitement. He drove around Hyson Green and Forest Fields before crossing Gregory Boulevard and entering Radford's maze of small streets. It was there that he first sighted the young couple strolling together along Alfreton Road. It was the girl who drew his attention; dressed in pink and wearing white socks, she looked no more than twelve.

Turning round, Black drove back and saw that the couple had separated. He was in time to glimpse the girl turning into a side street; turning back he followed her. After driving past her he pulled into the kerb on the opposite side of the road. Getting out, Black went to the front of the van and lifted the bonnet; with his head buried he watched the girl as she drew level on the other side of the road. 'Oi!' he shouted across to her.

Teresa and Andrew had parted company at the end of Norton Street. A few moments later she was overtaken by a blue van which drew up ahead of her on the other side of the road. Funny, she was certain that she had seen the van a few minutes earlier while still with Andrew. Teresa saw the driver get out, walk round to the front of the vehicle and lift up the bonnet. As she drew level she heard him call across to her, 'Oi, can you fix engines?' With her heart starting to pound, she ignored the question and quickened her pace.

Without warning a pair of thick arms were round her, grasping her tightly against a fat, soft belly. She opened her mouth to scream, but before she could do so the man moved an arm up and clamped it across her mouth; at the same time he lifted her bodily off her feet and started to carry her across the road towards the van. He was breathing hard and she could smell his reeking breath, while his body smelt of grime and sweat.

Teresa saw the gaping side opening in the van and knew that once inside there would be no escape. With the realisation came a determination not to be taken, and she started to fight and struggle as never before. Kicking, wriggling and straining against the vice-like hold, she could see the hole in the side of the van getting nearer, waiting to engulf her. Then he was trying to push her inside; with a supreme effort she managed to hook a leg under the door sill. The man tried to tug her away, in doing so relaxing slightly the suffocating grip he had across her mouth. It was the opportunity Teresa needed; opening her mouth she bit deep into the muscle of his right forearm. Her attacker gasped with pain and wrenched his arm away. Another half-chance for his victim. 'Mum, mum!' she screamed with all the force she could muster from her oxygen-starved lungs.

A hundred and fifty yards away Andrew Beeston heard Teresa scream. Something was wrong; racing back round the corner into Norton Street he saw the struggle going on further up the road. Charging along the last few yards he yelled at the man holding his friend, 'Let go of her, you fat git!'

Teresa heard Andrew as did her assailant, causing him to redouble his efforts to get her into the van. Still Teresa resisted with her leg hooked round the door sill. She could feel herself weakening and knew that she could not hold out much longer. With her free hand she groped behind her and found his crotch. Instinctively she squeezed with all her remaining strength. She heard the man grunt loudly in agony. 'You . . . bitch,' he snarled as, releasing her to hold his testicles, he lurched round to the driver's door.

Teresa collapsed into the roadway as the van engine fired and the vehicle jerked away. Andrew helped her to her feet and with the girl sobbing hysterically, together they part stumbled, part ran to her home.

Black was shaken; he had never experienced anything like it. As he drove as fast as he dared along Western Boulevard to Wollaton Road and then out of Nottingham towards the M1, he thought back over what had just taken place. It had promised to be a straightforward snatch and by now he should have been on his way with the kid in the back. Instead he was haring out of Nottingham with nothing to show for his efforts except a bloodied arm and a pair of aching balls. The girl had certainly decided that she wasn't going with him. None of the others had fought like her or had her strength. The boy's arrival had spoilt everything; even if he had managed to get the girl into the van and driven off, the laddie would have raised the alarm within minutes and every copper for miles would by now have been on the look-out for him. They still might be if either of them had thought to take the number of his van.

Black's concern over this last point was needless. Both Teresa Thornhill and Andrew Beeston had been so shocked by what had happened that neither had thought of making a note of the van's number. Instead their only thought was to get to the safety of Teresa's home as quickly as possible.

When their sobbing and hysterical daughter arrived home with Andrew, Brian and Ruby Thornhill had listened horrified as the young couple blurted out what had taken place. Brian immediately telephoned the police, informing them of what had happened, and giving as much information about his daughter's assailant and his vehicle as she and Andrew could recall. As Black had surmised, police immediately passed details on to their mobile units, but already it was too late. Their quarry was speeding down the M1 motorway towards London.

The next day Detective Chief Inspector Bruce Foster voiced police concern over the attack when he told the *Nottingham Evening Post*: 'This was a horrifying assault . . . We are obviously very anxious to catch this man because if he had succeeded in getting her into the van we could have been dealing with a much more serious offence.'

Crucially no connection was made between the Nottingham attack and the murders of Susan Maxwell, Caroline Hogg and Sarah Harper, and so Hector Clark and his team were not informed of the attempted abduction of the Nottingham girl until after Black's arrest two years later.

Looking back this appears to have been a strange omission. Apart from the similarities surrounding this assault and those on Maxwell, Hogg and Harper, including the resemblance between the victims and the use of a Transit-type van, the Nottingham attack should have struck a chord in the memory of the local police following the recovery two years before of Sarah Harper's body from the River Trent, less than 2 miles distant.

During the following weeks Nottingham Police mounted a full-scale investigation to trace the man who had attempted to abduct Teresa Thornhill. However, as various leads petered out the inquiry was gradually run down. It was only after Robert Black's arrest in July 1990 that a connection was made between him and the Thornhill attack. During the inquiry that intensified after Black had started to serve his life sentence, irrefutable circumstantial evidence emerged that put Black in Nottingham about an hour before the attack on Teresa Thornhill, and again three days later when he returned to the city.

CHAPTER 10

CAPTURED

Robert Black was on his way home. Things had started to go wrong in Edinburgh when he had collided with a bus at a roundabout. Nothing serious, just a dent in his front wing, but the incident had left him in a bad mood. Since then, however, as he drove south the urge had been growing on him. He had been on a regular, bonus-earning Scottish delivery run and was now driving south along the familiar A7 towards the border. It was Saturday, 14 July 1990, a hot sunny day on which already he had seen several small girls wearing provocative summer dresses, increasing the compelling demand within him.

He passed the signpost for Stow and shortly afterwards entered the village. He already knew the place; nothing much there apart from a couple of shops, a café and a church. As he cruised through the village he spotted a girl of eleven or twelve walking along the pavement ahead of him. He drew up alongside her, slowed down and opened the passenger door. 'Is there a café around here, lassie?' he asked her across the passenger seat. Once she came close enough he could grab her and yank her into his van. The girl looked startled and then apprehensive as he spoke to her, but before she could reply or approach him a large Golden Retriever ran up, wagging his tail and barking. The girl had a quick word with the dog who stopped barking. Black, not wishing to draw attention to himself by antagonising the animal, engaged gear and continued along the road.

He decided to call in at the café, which he had used on previous occasions, for a bite to eat and to contemplate his next move. After buying a newspaper from a shop opposite, he chose a seat by the window from where he could watch the road. A little girl passed; pretty little thing, he thought to himself as he watched her disappear round a corner further up the road.

Black left the café and continued through the village, keeping an eye open for a likely target. His earlier aborted attempt had set his adrenalin pumping and his urge was now overwhelming. For a few minutes he drove round, conscious that despite the urgency of his demands he could not remain too long in the village without attracting attention. He had decided to abandon his quest and had stopped near the centre of the village to wipe over his windscreen when he spotted her. A few yards up the road a little blonde-haired girl about six years old stepped out of a driveway and turned towards him.

It was the opportunity Robert Black had been seeking; moving swiftly round to the nearside of his van, he opened the passenger door and waited as the girl approached. As she drew level with his van Black stooped down and with a single movement swept her up and pushed her through the passenger door on to the floor of the Transit. Climbing through after her he slid across to the driver's seat and started the engine. Doing a brisk three-point turn, he sped off towards Edinburgh, his surprised and terrified victim cowering down in the passenger well, too frightened even to scream.

Robert Black drove out of Stow looking for a suitable place in which to stop. Two miles along the road he found what he was seeking: an unoccupied lay-by where a stationary van would not attract undue notice.

Back in the village there was considerable activity. Black would have been surprised and concerned had he known that his recent deed had been witnessed. David Herkes, a fifty-six-year-old former sub-postmaster, had taken advantage of the fine weather to mow his front lawn. Pausing briefly to adjust the blades of his mower, he noticed Mandy Wilson, a neighbour's daughter, emerge from the driveway of a house opposite. He watched her disappear behind a stationary van, the driver of which appeared to be polishing the windscreen. As Herkes bent down he could see her legs together with those of the driver who had moved to the nearside of the vehicle. Suddenly the little girl's legs disappeared as she was lifted from the pavement. At the same time he could see the van driver apparently trying to push something through the passenger door before clambering over into his seat and starting up the engine.

Herkes watched this activity, which occupied only a few seconds, with growing disbelief. As the van did a three-point turn before it accelerated away towards Edinburgh he scribbled down the vehicle's registration number, certain that he had just witnessed the abduction of his little neighbour. He then ran the few yards to Mandy Wilson's home where he rapidly explained to her mother what he had seen. Mrs Wilson did not hesitate; immediately she dialled 999 and informed the police of what had recently taken place.

Normally the area around Stow is not heavily policed, but on this day in July 1990, there were several more police vehicles in the vicinity than was usual. A car rally 20 miles away at Kelso may have accounted for the extra police presence, but whatever the reason within minutes of receiving the emergency call half a dozen police vehicles had arrived in the village. They were met by David Herkes, Mandy Wilson's distraught father and a number of other villagers who had assembled at the scene.

It is a truism often quoted in crime stories that a murderer invariably makes a crucial mistake that leads to his unmasking. How else would detectives such as Holmes, Poirot and Morse succeed so regularly in solving their cases? Not by the painstaking, tedious and often lengthy methods employed by real-life detectives; much too uninspired. Nonetheless many a notorious killer has made a vital mistake that has led to their capture.

Such an example was that of Robert Black. On that summer afternoon he was travelling *south* along the A7 towards Galashiels where he was due to make his next delivery. Why then did he decide to drive *north* out of Stow after he had snatched his victim? Was he disorientated? This appears an unlikely explanation as he was very familiar with the A7 and would have been aware of which direction to travel. Had he recalled the lay-by that he must have passed earlier, noting its convenience? Equally improbable, as when passing the lay-by it is doubtful he would have foreseen the events that were soon to take place. In any case he would almost certainly have come across an equally suitable stopping place for his purpose during the 6 miles between the village and Galashiels.

I suggest the most likely explanation is that Black, anxious to get away from Stow as quickly as possible, and experiencing the stress and sexual excitement that accompanied his recent activity, had driven his van blindly out of the village either without caring or without being immediately aware of the direction in which he was travelling. Later, during or immediately following his assault on Mandy Wilson, he realised that he was facing in the opposite direction to that of his proposed route, prompting his decision to drive back through Stow. This was either sheer foolhardiness, or done with a feeling of immunity; having got away with things for so long, why should today be any different? He was soon to find out.

He sped down the A7 and re-entered Stow. Too late he saw his mistake

and with it came the realisation that his days of fulfilment at the expense
of little girls were about to end. Ahead of him several police vehicles were
haphazardly parked, their occupants mingling with a crowd of villagers
in the middle of the road. As he drove towards them Black did not hear
David Herkes cry out, 'That's the same van, that's the same van.' He was
conscious only of a uniformed policeman, his arm raised, stepping out in
front of him just yards away. Instinctively he braked and his van slewed to
a halt. After that all was confusion.

Mandy Wilson's father had accompanied David Herkes back to the
scene of his daughter's abduction to await the police arrival. Soon afterwards when the first police car drove up Herkes described to the policeman what he had witnessed, and gave him a description of the man and
his vehicle. As he was speaking more police vehicles arrived in response
to the emergency call; soon they were joined by several villagers, drawn
to the scene by the activity.

While police were relaying the information to their Edinburgh control
room for circulation to other units, to adjoining regions and to neighbouring forces in England, a relative of the Wilsons' arrived. He said that,
a short while before, he had seen a blue van stationary in a lay-by a couple
of miles along the Edinburgh road. Officers hastened to impart this
information to colleagues heading towards Stow, but their efforts were to
prove unnecessary.

David Herkes could scarcely believe it when he saw, approaching from
the northern end of the village, the same van that he had seen earlier.
'That's the same van, that's the same van,' he shouted out, pointing at the
Transit. A uniformed police constable stepped in front of the approaching vehicle and raised his arm, signalling to the driver to stop. He braked
sharply and stopped a yard in front of the officer.

Several policemen converged on the driver and hauled him out of his
seat and into the road. As they were doing so, Mandy Wilson's father
climbed into the van's gloomy interior. At first he could see no sign of his
daughter, only what appeared to be a bundle of rags against the partition
dividing the rear of the van from the driver's compartment. He called out
her name and saw a slight movement from the bundle. He went closer and
saw that it was not rags, but a crumpled sleeping bag. He untied the draw-
string and opened it up; inside lay his daughter, hands tied behind her
back, legs bound together and with a hood over her head. Loosening and
removing the hood and releasing her hands, the girl's father was greeted
by a terrified look from his daughter who was unable to speak due to a

length of sticking plaster that was taped across her mouth. 'Mandy was fully conscious but petrified . . .' Mr Wilson told reporters as he relived the moment he first set eyes on his daughter in the back of the Transit.

After she had been lifted gently out of the van, Mandy and her father were met by her mother who had arrived on the scene. As he stepped away from the vehicle, Mr Wilson noticed Black standing handcuffed at the rear. 'That's my daughter, you bastard,' Wilson spat out. 'I will never forget that image of him. From that alone there would be no problem identifying him,' he said later.

Together he and his wife carefully removed the sticking plaster from Mandy Wilson's red and swollen face. Clinging to them both, her body damp with sweat, the terrified little girl appeared at first to be physically unharmed. It was only the subsequent doctor's examination that revealed the full nature of the horrendous sexual attack to which she had been subjected.

Black meanwhile was hustled across to a police car where he was put into a rear seat alongside Detective Sergeant William Ormiston. During the journey to Selkirk police station, Black made the first of the few remarks he was ever to make to police.

'What a day it's been. It should have happened on Friday the 13th . . .' he said.

Friday the 13th or Saturday the 14th, the result was the same – Robert Black's eight-year reign of death and depravity had been brought to an end.

CHAPTER 11

LIFE

On the way back to Selkirk police station Black spoke again to Sergeant Ormiston. 'It must have been a sudden rush of blood to the head,' he said, before admitting, 'I have always been interested in young girls since I was a lad.' He added casually that he had only touched his latest victim 'a little', and that he had intended to take her to somewhere 'like Blackpool' where he could spend more time with her.

After Black arrived at the police station no time was lost in notifying Detective Superintendent Andrew Watt who was the weekend duty superintendent at Edinburgh, available to deal initially with any major crime that occurred within the force area. Watt drove immediately to Selkirk and attempted to interview the prisoner regarding the abduction, but found him reluctant to answer questions. Despite this, when informed of the circumstances Watt soon perceived a similarity between the Stow abduction and those of Susan Maxwell, Caroline Hogg and Sarah Harper, and realised that they may have netted a very big fish indeed.

The evidence against Black in the latest case was overwhelming. There was an eyewitness to the abduction; Mandy Wilson had been found by her father bound and gagged in the back of his van; the vehicle had been spotted in a lay-by a couple of miles away; and he had been stopped while driving it back past the scene of the abduction.

After written statements had been made by the arresting officers, Black was charged with plagium, the Scottish equivalent of abduction. Pending his appearance at Selkirk Sheriff court on Monday morning, he was left to ponder over his situation in a cell at the police station. Meanwhile Hector Clark was informed of the arrest.

When Clark arrived at Selkirk on Monday morning he met Robert Black briefly for the first time. He felt instinctively that the man sitting morosely before him, giving monosyllabic replies to his innocuous questions, was the man he and his team had sought for so long.

As is customary in Scotland, the first remand hearing was heard later that Monday morning behind closed doors. Afterwards Black was conveyed the 30 or so miles to the grim Victorian confines of Saughton Prison in Edinburgh where he was to spend the next seven days. Hector Clark meanwhile deputed Detective Superintendent Andrew Watt and Detective Chief Inspector Roger Orr, both from the Lothian and Borders force, to seek out evidence linking Robert Black with the child murders. This was to prove to be a far more formidable task than was envisaged at the outset.

With Black in custody, police immediately set about the process that was to culminate four years later in Newcastle Crown Court. The immediate job was to prepare the Stow case for the High Court in Edinburgh. The Scottish rule that restricts the period a prisoner may spend in custody between his arrest and trial to 110 days, ensures that neither the prosecution nor the defence delay unnecessarily in preparing their cases. The Stow abduction case kept well within that limit; Black was to spend only twenty-seven days in custody from the day of his arrest until his appearance in the High Court.

Matters were expedited by the defence giving notice to the prosecution by what in Scotland is known as a 'Section 102 letter', that Black intended to plead guilty. As he had been caught virtually red-handed, and there was an eyewitness to the abduction, the defence move was foreseeable; a further consideration may have been a remote hope on Black's part that by pleading guilty and thus avoiding the necessity of calling witnesses to give harrowing testimony, he may have been rewarded with a lighter sentence.

Concomitant with these early manoeuvrings, on 27 July 1990, senior detectives from the six forces involved in the investigation met in Edinburgh. After a summary had been given of the inquiry, culminating in Robert Black's arrest, the meeting was thrown open to ideas and suggestions as to how the investigation should progress. A lively discussion followed in which criticism of certain aspects of the inquiry were aired, along with proposals about future advances. By the end of the meeting much useful information had been circulated, ideas exchanged, and the way forward more clearly defined.

Early in their current investigation the Scottish detectives contacted the Metropolitan Police and asked them to visit 31 West Bank, Stamford Hill, to see if a search there would reveal any incriminating material. The result far exceeded their expectations; a thorough search of Black's former room disclosed a wealth of pornographic books, videos and photographs, together with a variety of both purpose-designed and adapted sex aids. Significantly child pornography featured largely in the collection.

When the room had been cleared, all the material was parcelled up and sent to Edinburgh where the gymnasium at the force headquarters in Fettes Avenue had been commandeered to accommodate it. Meanwhile Home Office forensic experts and police photographers moved into 31 West Bank; while the scientists meticulously examined Black's accommodation for traces that could later be used in evidence, photographers took pictures and filmed both the inside and outside of the house.

Robert Black's Transit van had also been cleared out. The assorted ropes, sticking plaster, hoods and girls' clothing, together with a selection of sexual aids, left police in no doubt as to the use to which the vehicle had been put, or the kind of man that was in custody. By this time Hector Clark and his colleagues were confident that Robert Black was the man responsible for the Maxwell, Hogg and Harper crimes. The task of proving their instincts still lay ahead.

As evidence was gathered in and an increasing number of people provided information about Black's employment and social background, it soon became apparent that the inquiries were to be both lengthy and involved. A special incident room was set up at St Leonard's police station on Edinburgh's south side which was to be the base for the ongoing investigation.

The Maxwell, Hogg and Harper families had been informed of Robert Black's arrest at Stow, and of police suspicion that he was the man they had been seeking for abducting and murdering their children. The Hoggs declined to make any public comment on receiving the news. Elizabeth Maxwell's thoughts on hearing of the discovery of Mandy Wilson by her father in the back of Black's van had flown back to the terror and bewilderment her own daughter must have experienced at the time of her abduction. 'Her last thoughts must have been, "Why are my mummy and daddy not coming?"' she said.

Jackie Harper, by 1990 engaged to a former military policeman who had been one of the 2000 sympathisers and well-wishers who had contacted her after the death of Sarah, was forthright in expressing her feelings: 'I can't think properly about my own future while he is still free . . .

Please God it's the breakthrough the police have been waiting for.' Thoughts of her daughter were also never far from her mind. 'Sarah would have been fifteen next month and she is always in our thoughts, particularly around her birthdays . . . Only when the killer is caught will the pain and sadness of the last few years be over.'

While Black was on remand in Saughton Prison during July and August 1990, the Edinburgh Procurator Fiscal ordered that a psychiatric assessment of the accused man be carried out for his information. A second examination commissioned by the defence was to be done and a report prepared for the information of the trial judge. Both assessments were undertaken by eminent psychiatrists, Dr Baird from the Carstairs Hospital in Lanark for the Fiscal, Dr Zealley, consultant psychiatrist at the Royal Edinburgh Hospital's Mental Health Unit, for the judge. Both reports were uncompromising regarding Black's deviancy and his proclivities towards young children, and did nothing to encourage the judge towards leniency.

On Friday, 10 August 1990, less than a month after his arrest, Robert Black sat in the High Court, which is situated within the precincts of the Parliament House and which was until the signing of the Treaty of Union with England in 1707 the seat of the Scottish parliament. Facing him sat the Right Honourable Lord Donald MacArthur Ross, the Lord Justice Clerk, Scotland's second most senior judge. Black was represented by Mr Herbert Kerrigan QC, with Scotland's Lord Advocate, Lord Fraser of Carmylie QC, personally leading for the prosecution.

The court room was crowded as the case had attracted considerable publicity with the press having already caught on to the fact that a man in custody in Scotland was being investigated regarding the three child murders. Black was brought into the dock where he sat flanked by two white-gloved policemen. 'Call the Diet, Her Majesty's Advocate against Robert Black' directed the Clerk of the Court.

Members of the public gazed at Black while reporters busily took notes as Mr Kerrigan stood up and announced that he appeared for the accused who was pleading guilty to the charges on the indictment. It was then the turn of the Lord Advocate to outline the facts of the case. In a modulated voice, Lord Fraser described how Black had been seen in the act of abducting Mandy Wilson; her ordeal in the back of the van; and how Black's fortuitous arrest in Stow was followed by the discovery of the little girl by her father.

Those in court had listened silently as the prosecutor continued by referring the judge to the psychiatrist's report, concluding his address by moving for sentence. After Lord Fraser finished speaking it was again the turn of Herbert Kerrigan, this time to speak in mitigation. He made the most of what little there was for him to draw upon. He told the court that his client insisted that this was an isolated incident, and that there had been no intention of killing the child. He went on to say that Black admitted having been previously tempted, but until this occasion had resisted the temptation. The defence advocate said that Black now accepted that he was a danger and wished to undertake some form of treatment.

When Mr Kerrigan sat down it remained only for Lord Ross to pronounce sentence. That Black would go to prison there was no doubt; the question was for how long? Before sentencing Black the Judge paid tribute to David Herkes whose vigilance and prompt action on that July afternoon had been almost entirely responsible for Black's arrest. He then went on: 'The abduction of this little girl was carried out with chilling, cold calculation. This was no "rush of blood" as you have claimed.' Saying that he was bound to be greatly influenced by the opinion of the psychiatrist who adjudged that Black was, and would continue to be, a serious danger to children, the Lord Advocate told him that a custodial sentence was the only safe option. 'You will go to prison for life and your release will not be considered until such a time as it is safe to do so.'

As Hector Clark, Andrew Watt and Roger Orr left the Parliament House amid the scurry of reporters anxious to get the story back to their editors in time for the next edition, this sentence for the policemen signalled the end of only part of the case against Robert Black. During the days that followed as he thought matters over in Saughton Prison, Black may have been hoping that he had escaped the consequences of his worst excesses. If so he was to be disappointed. For Hector Clark and the other detectives, the challenge remained for them to nail responsibility for the deaths of Susan Maxwell, Caroline Hogg and Sarah Harper on the man starting his life sentence. They were under no illusion as to the complexity of the task confronting them; even so they would probably still have been confounded had they known that it was to be almost four years before Robert Black once more stood in the dock.

Less than a month after their client had been given his life sentence, Robert Black's lawyers lodged notice of appeal against the sentence. To assist them they arranged for an independent psychiatric examination to be carried out in the hope that its findings would enable them to rebut the pre-trial examination reports compiled by Dr Baird and Dr Zealley which together had been instrumental in Black being sent to prison for life.

The report was prepared by the Director of the Gracewell Clinic in Birmingham, an establishment that was building a considerable reputation for its success in encouraging sexual offenders to confront their behaviour. Ray Wyre twice visited Robert Black in Saughton Prison where they had two long interviews. Despite having been engaged by the defence, Wyre's report was uncompromisingly frank in its assessment of Black and did nothing to raise hopes that the appeal would be successful. On the advice of his lawyers Black therefore agreed at the last minute to abandon the appeal. However, more was to be heard of Ray Wyre.

In November 1990, three months after being sentenced, Robert Black was transferred from Saughton Prison in Edinburgh to an establishment with a previously fearsome reputation 130 miles away in Aberdeenshire. Peterhead Prison had become synonymous with outbreaks of violence and rioting by inmates who were reputedly some of the toughest and most recalcitrant men in Scotland. However its ethos was changing; from being a prison in which men took a perverse pride in serving their sentence, enhancing as it did their reputation on the outside for hardness, it had become a major holding establishment for sexually convicted prisoners. Most of these would certainly hesitate later before letting it be known that they had spent time there.

Nevertheless the prison was developing a far different reputation from the one it had previously held among those having regular contact with sex offenders. Its imaginative approach, range of expertise and treatment options, and its view that sex offenders should not only be punished, but encouraged also to confront their deviancy and criminal behaviour, were finding increasing favour among some criminologists and others in the field of sexual psychology. It was hoped that in the long term such an approach would result in the offender changing for the better. It was within the walls of Her Majesty's Prison Peterhead that Robert Black was to spend the next four years.

CHAPTER 12

THE INTERVIEW

With Robert Black safely locked up following his arrest at Stow, Hector Clark and his team of detectives were faced with their greatest challenge. All of them were convinced that in Black they had the man responsible for the deaths of Susan Maxwell in 1982, Caroline Hogg in 1983 and Sarah Harper in 1986. Now they had to prove it.

Inquiries among his former workmates, friends and acquaintances with whom he had socialised, and the Raysons, together with the study of official records dating back to his birth, including a considerable amount of data gathered from the Social Services and Education Departments about his early days before leaving Scotland, had provided considerable information about his pre-adulthood and more recent background; none of it however, had any evidential value, or helped to connect him with the murders.

As a first step towards rectifying this, Hector Clark decided that Black should be intensively questioned by two of his most experienced detectives. Detective Superintendent Andrew Watt and Detective Chief Inspector Roger Orr had already spent some considerable time in preparing the Stow abduction case for trial and were thoroughly familiar with the investigation.

For reasons peculiar to Scotland's legal system it was decided that Robert Black should be questioned under the provisions of Section 2 of Scotland's Criminal Justice Act. In effect this limited the length of time Black could be detained for interviewing to six hours despite the fact that he was already in prison. Andrew Watt and Roger Orr had therefore to plan their interview very carefully; they had to ensure that each question was formulated in a way that encouraged a response, while extreme care had to be taken to avoid mentioning the circumstances of his current conviction, or referring to any of his other convictions for fear of prejudicing future proceedings against him.

The interview was to be conducted at Edinburgh's St Leonard's police station, and it was there on 23 August that Black was conveyed after having been collected by detectives from Saughton Prison. They were accompanied by a senior prison officer, for Black was now the responsibility of the Prison Department. At the police station he was taken up to an interview room equipped with tape-recording apparatus; there the two sides prepared for a lengthy interrogation session.

It had been decided by Andrew Watt and Roger Orr that their questioning of Black would work round to the Caroline Hogg murder. The primary reason for this decision was that the Hogg case was the one where suspicion of Black was strongest. A man closely resembling him had been spotted by several reliable witnesses, either on his own in Portobello, or in the company of a little girl. The second reason was that, as the abduction had taken place within the Lothian and Borders Police area, it was the case with which Watt and Orr were most familiar.

At 9 a.m. on Thursday, 23 August 1990, the two Scottish detectives sat down at a table in the interview room at St Leonard's police station. Facing them was the man that for the past eight years four, and later six, police forces had been hunting. The first thing that struck both policemen was the 'ordinariness' of the man opposite. Powerfully built, he was of medium height, balding, with a short greying beard and moustache; he gazed at them warily, although with a somewhat quizzical expression.

With only six hours in which to question Black, the two detectives launched immediately into their assignment. The first part of the interview was more of a discussion than an interrogation. In a quiet Scottish accent, Black spoke freely of his years in Kinlochleven. He mentioned in particular the profound effect the death of his long-time fostermother Betty Tulip had had upon him. He said that from being a confident extrovert, after her death he became inward-looking and withdrawn. This vision of himself did not tally with the impression he had created among several of his contemporaries who had later voiced their opinions to the police.

This may have been an attempt to convey the impression that his deviancy and offending pattern had been born of events in his early life, and could have been a deliberate ploy on Robert Black's part. His intelligence was not to be underestimated and he possibly thought that if he was able to convince the authorities, including the police, of the psychological harm that had resulted from the various upheavals in his early life, it might lead to a more relaxed prison regime.

This was further evidenced when Black went on to speak of his adolescence, the events that had occurred at the mixed-sex children's home at Redding, and, more particularly, the abuse he had been subjected to at the hands of the staff member at Musselburgh.

There seemed to be no aspect of his early years that Black was not prepared to discuss with Andrew Watt and Roger Orr. His early sexual experiences; experiments in various forms of self-abuse; his growing attraction towards young children, in particular females; the aborted relationship with Pamela Hodgson. All of these topics, and others, he uninhibitedly spoke about without any apparent self-consciousness.

After a while Watt and Orr, conscious of the time span into which their questioning had to be confined, referred back to Black's life at Musselburgh, his feeling of being trapped while being abused, and his feelings of powerlessness at not being able to do anything about it.

Black similarly enlarged on other aspects of his early life. The fantasies that accompanied his self-abuse; his penchant for wearing young girls' clothing and swimsuits and the satisfaction he obtained from his bizarre liking for inserting a variety of household implements into his rectum. To all of these admissions Andrew Watt and Roger Orr listened without betraying any sign of distaste or revulsion, reactions which could have resulted in Black curtailing his more lurid and revealing admissions.

During the course of the interview the detectives varied their technique to encourage truthful replies to their questions. They had made it clear from the start that they were in no way judgemental, and sought only to discover what motivated Black into his aberrant behaviour, including experiences that had contributed towards it.

So far everything had gone pretty well according to their pre-arranged plan. Watt and Orr had succeeded in painting a clear picture of the man whom they were interviewing. However, when they attempted to steer the discussion into areas more relevant to their current inquiries, Black's openness in replying to questions began to evaporate.

The detectives showed him some of the pornographic self-portraits he had taken, and followed this up by talking about the dozens of innocuous photographs he had taken of children at the seaside. As they continued to talk about children they gradually introduced the subject of abduction.

It was done subtly; they spoke first about his employment background and his last job with PDS, one that he had enjoyed. The various alternative routes across England and Scotland, and his regular habit of visiting

John and Angela Rayson at their Donisthorpe home, were also brought up. Finally, with two-thirds of their permitted time with Black having elapsed, Watt and Orr raised the subject of Caroline Hogg's abduction. Andrew Watt informed Black that police had already established that he was in Portobello on the day Caroline was abducted. Careful not to reveal too much, Black's interviewers showed him a petrol receipt which he had signed which proved he had purchased fuel at Belford, south of the English/Scottish border, on 8 July 1983. They also produced photographs of him which, when compared to the police artist's drawing prepared from witnesses' impressions, showed there to be a remarkable likeness.

Sensing the tenor that the interview was taking, Black's replies, from being neither restrained nor inhibited, became monosyllabic. As I have mentioned, Robert Black was far from being unintelligent and now steadfastly defied the best efforts of Andrew Watt and Roger Orr to persuade him to confess to the murders of Caroline Hogg, Susan Maxwell or Sarah Harper. Neither when told that police and many other people were convinced of his guilt, nor when they appealed to him to end the suffering being endured by the girls' families, did he respond.

Despite the fact that he was already in prison serving a life sentence, for reasons of his own Robert Black appeared determined not to give detectives the slightest assistance towards what he shrewdly judged would be the formidable task of gathering sufficient evidence with which to have him convicted of the murders.

After Black had departed at the end of the interview, Andrew Watt and Roger Orr felt mentally exhausted as they reflected on what had been achieved. They were both more than ever convinced that they had spent six hours in the company of the man responsible for the deaths of the three girls. However, apart from providing an even deeper insight into Robert Black's psyche, the interview had done little to advance the murder inquiry. They knew that Black's conviction for the murders would only be brought about if enough evidence could be obtained to prove his indisputable guilt. After so many years it was a daunting but challenging prospect.

Being convinced of Robert Black's guilt was one thing; gathering enough evidence to justify taking him back to court on charges of abduction and murder was quite another. Up until Black's arrest and conviction for the Stow abduction there had been few positive leads; the inquiry had been merely ticking over in the hope that eventually something would emerge, or an incident would occur that would provide justification for reactivating the inquiry. With the arrest of Robert Black such a development had arisen.

The circumstances of the Stow abduction, and subsequent inquiries following his arrest, pointed unerringly at Black as the perpetrator of the earlier crimes. Even so, evidence connecting him with the abductions and murders of Susan Maxwell, Caroline Hogg and Sarah Harper was still lacking. There had been hopes that Detective Superintendent Andrew Watt's and Detective Chief Inspector Roger Orr's interview with Black might have advanced the inquiry, or even encouraged a confession. It had done neither, merely reinforcing the strong suspicion they had that he was their man.

The murder investigation that was led by detectives from Lothian and Borders and Staffordshire Police under Andrew Watt, Roger Orr and Peter Herward must rank as one of the longest and most complicated in the annals of British policing.

Preliminary inquiries had already been made of Black's former employers, Poster Dispatch and Storage in East London, mainly to confirm the period that Black had been in their employ. It had emerged during those inquiries that his job had taken him the length and breadth of England and Scotland. If it could be proved that Black had been in the vicinity at the time of the Maxwell, Hogg and Harper abductions, or at the time their bodies were dumped many miles away, detectives would be that much closer to associating him with the crimes.

The foremost problem confronting police was from where, after so many years, could such evidence be obtained? Detectives went back to PDS to question again the office staff and drivers, many of whom had been at the company at the same time as Robert Black. Some of the information the detectives were seeking was contained in wages books going back to the early 1980s retained by the company. For several days they pored over these books and scrutinised pay slips until eventually they were satisfied that Black had been on the Scottish run between Thursday, 29 July and Wednesday, 4 August 1982. It was an encouraging discovery but was only part of what the detectives needed to know. It still had to be proved that Black was near Coldstream, and at what time on Friday, 30 July, the day that Susan Maxwell had vanished. The process would then have to be repeated in the cases of Caroline Hogg and Sarah Harper.

The early inquiries to reconstruct precisely Robert Black's movements on the days that Susan Maxwell, Caroline Hogg and Sarah Harper were abducted were made by detectives from Lothian and Borders. Although they were soon able to establish that Black had been nearby when the abductions had occurred, it was the time that was difficult to adduce. There would be little value in just knowing that Robert Black was in Scotland on 30 July 1982, or even that he was in the Borders region on that day, without being able to prove as accurately as possible the time that he was there. This applied equally to the Portobello and Morley abductions.

After having made exhaustive studies of the wages books and pay slips at PDS, and having spoken with those of the company's staff who could explain the complexities of the overtime and bonus systems, and how from those figures, the length and duration of a driver's journey could be deduced, the Scottish detectives sought ways of utilising their knowledge to establish the exact time Black was at a specific location.

It was at this point that they learnt that, in common with many companies, PDS had accounts with several oil companies which enabled drivers of company vehicles to purchase fuel without cash changing hands. The agency card with which each driver was provided had a similar function to that of the familiar bank credit card, except that its use was restricted to obtaining vehicle fuel and lubricants.

At this stage of the inquiry Staffordshire detectives joined forces with their colleagues from Lothian and Borders. The Scottish officers, including Detective Constables Lindsey McBride, Tom Bell and Alan Cossar working under the direction of Andrew Watt and Roger Orr, had already crated over 5000 exhibits removed from Black's flat. These were now stored in sterile conditions together with his clothing, awaiting a full forensic examination which was to be carried out by scientists from Edinburgh and Aberdeen.

From 1990 one of the most involved and protracted aspects of the inquiry was that of tracing Robert Black's fuel purchases on his journeys to Scotland in July 1982 and July 1983, and to the north of England, including Leeds, in 1986. Deputed to carry out part of this inquiry was a small team of Staffordshire detectives under the leadership of Detective Inspector Peter Herward. Detective Constable Tony Beardmore went first to Edinburgh to discover what line of inquiry the Staffordshire team should pursue. It was decided that they should concentrate on the petrol agency cards.

Returning to Poster Dispatch and Storage the Staffordshire detectives at first met with little success. They were informed that the company had dealt solely with British Petroleum and that all records relating to agency card transactions in 1982 had been destroyed. Further probing, however, revealed that in fact PDS had credit arrangements also with the Shell, Fina and Mobil oil companies. Of these Mobil, they were informed, would probably prove to be the most co-operative and rewarding.

Beardmore travelled down to Mobil's head office in Victoria Street, London. He spent five weeks there absorbing details of how the agency system operated. However, he was unable to examine tickets, dockets and other relevant documentation as the Mobil administration department was at Sevenoaks in Kent. The detective went to Sevenoaks only to discover two days after his arrival that the department was being transferred to Maidstone. Mindful of the crucial importance to the murder inquiry of many of the thousands of documents to be moved, Beardmore approached the manager overseeing the move to emphasise to him the importance of the material to the police, in particular the microfilm of the tickets, dockets and slips, and to ask him to try and ensure that none of it was lost or mislaid. His request was heeded and not a single relevant item went missing during the move.

It was with Mobil Oil that Tony Beardmore gained his initial success. With minor variations, the method of operating the agency system of cards and dockets is very similar throughout the oil industry. Nevertheless each company jealously guards the secrets of its operations. It is to the credit of the detectives engaged on the task of retracing Robert Black's routes, and establishing his whereabouts several years prior to their inquiries, that they should have succeeded in prising the necessary information from the oil companies.

Beardmore and his colleagues set about checking millions of fuel receipts stored at Mobil premises as far apart as Epsom and Stockport. This aspect of their investigation was unsuccessful, the detectives finding no evidence of fuel purchases made by Black at the time of Susan Maxwell's disappearance. However, they did gain considerable knowledge about the way in which the system operated. Armed with this information they next approached other oil companies, and it was with these that the information Beardmore and the others had obtained from Mobil proved its worth.

Several different departments in oil companies, including sales, VAT and off-shore, extract information from individual fuel dockets that is relevant to their own sphere of activity. The secrecy between companies extends to departments within those companies, each of which is careful to safeguard its own interests within the organisation.

At this stage of the investigation the Staffordshire detectives decided to concentrate on British Petroleum. They arrived at Hemel Hempstead to examine and analyse the information conveyed on millions of petrol dockets that was condensed into one line and transferred to thousands of forms AG30. Beardmore realised that if they could trace form AG30 for July 1982 it would provide 90 per cent of the information they were seeking. The only thing lacking would be Robert Black's signature.

The microfiched forms were taken back to the reopened incident room at Newcastle which was housed in the former court building. There, women police officers, some of whom had been involved in the 1982 Maxwell inquiry, spent several weeks scrutinising the millions of one-line entries on forms AG30, trying to find evidence of Robert Black's fuel purchases. In addition the women officers spent many hours on other aspects of the inquiry, including index searches for references to white vans, and relevant witness statements.

Each one-line entry on form AG30 contained a wealth of information: the date of the transaction, the name of the card holder, his company, the amount of fuel drawn, and its cost, the type of fuel purchased, i.e. 2-star, 4-star or diesel, and most important of all, the garage site number, which pin-pointed the location of every garage in the oil company's chain.

It was not enough to know that Black had obtained fuel at Garage X on a particular date; it had to be narrowed down as near as possible to the actual time the transaction took place. This proved to be a tedious, time-consuming procedure. Taking with them the agency company's credit sales slips, detectives visited dozens of garages and other fuel retail outlets at which Black was known to have obtained fuel. Sometimes these were situated at motorway service areas where it was also occasionally possible to establish that he had purchased refreshments.

In the majority of garages and other fuel outlets, similar problems were encountered: some employees had moved, some establishments had been taken over by different oil companies. Other garages had been sold out or had simply closed down. Despite such problems and setbacks, detectives countrywide persevered. Slowly their determination brought results. The occasional assistant acknowledged that they had completed a particular slip, and some were even able to recall what hours they had been working on a specific day. This in itself considerably narrowed down the time of purchase.

As Tony Beardmore, the Staffordshire detective who had been involved in the Susan Maxwell inquiry in 1982, pointed out: 'The problem we had with the Maxwell case was that we did not have a lot of evidence of Black's movements. It was the agency card investigation that eventually provided us with that evidence.'

There was a stroke of luck for Beardmore upon his arrival at BP. He learnt that a few days before the head of the agency department had instructed his assistant to destroy all correspondence and documentation appertaining to fuel transactions that had taken place before September 1982. VAT regulations required that such matters be retained for seven years; company policy dictated that it should be kept for a further year. Fortunately the departmental assistant head had not got round to complying with the instruction before Beardmore and his colleagues arrived, so material relating to July 1982 was still available.

The agency card sales slips were numbered sequentially; apart therefore from the references to Robert Black's purchases, the drivers who had bought fuel either side of Black were also traced and later interviewed. John Stanhope who lives in Manchester recalls: 'One day in late 1990 two detectives called on me. I almost laughed outright when they asked me if I could recall buying some petrol near Nottingham on a day back in 1986. But they questioned me very skilfully and as a result of that, and an association of ideas it built up, I surprised myself eventually by recalling the incident. It was very impressive.'

Other witnesses were unable to remember the time, but were able to say whether they had bought fuel in the morning or the afternoon. It all helped. This part of the investigation was tedious and time-consuming. After establishing the name of the company to which the fuel purchase had been invoiced, detectives had first to visit the company in a bid to ascertain the whereabouts of the person named on the docket; sometimes that person was still involved with the company. More frequently the purchaser had left the firm, or the company no longer existed. This entailed further lengthy inquiries which if successful led to them being interviewed.

Detective Constables Beardmore and Leighton recalled their elation when microfiche covering the period of Susan Maxwell's abduction was found. The fiche was stored in a room at the top of the BP building, while there was a microfiche viewer in the basement. This was sometimes used prior to sending the microfiched forms AG30 back to the Newcastle incident room for closer examination and analysis by women officers.

'It was the most exciting moment of my life,' said Beardmore. 'When we stood in that office and looked at those films – it's hard to explain the feeling to anyone who was not actively involved. We rushed down to the basement and verified it on the machine. It was then that we fully realised that those rows of figures told us what we wanted to know, where Robert Black got petrol before picking our girl [Maxwell] up . . . having found one, we had to go on and find the others.'

Tony Leighton had been equally excited: 'I think it was the elation of finding the first one and realising what we could do. We knew that in another two or three months we would have found out all we needed to know.'

The breakthrough had come at the beginning of October. There was a vast amount of work to be completed before any thought could be given to preparing a case for consideration by the Crown Prosecution Service. An important advance had been achieved; it now remained a question of expanding on the evidence obtained and searching for more clues linking Black with the other cases.

Shortly after Black had been interviewed at St Leonard's police station, Hector Clark was notified of the aborted attempt that had been made to abduct Teresa Thornhill in Nottingham over two years previously. Why he had not been informed earlier is unclear. Following his appointment to head the joint inquiry, Clark had asked all Chief Constables to inform him of similar incidents involving children. Despite this request, details of the Teresa Thornhill case had never reached him. Following Robert Black's arrest both Clark and the Nottinghamshire force recognised that the incident could be vital to the inquiry and it became an integral part of the overall investigation.

Steady progress was being made as an increasing number of AG30s were studied and the information they contained was analysed. From time to time luck favoured the detectives; on one occasion, during an interview with a witness they had traced, he revealed that he had always kept a diary and was thus able to tell them that on a particular date at a specific time, he had been at a filling station immediately before Black had stopped there. Such pieces of good fortune were rare. Most of the time it was a tedious, unexciting task.

It is difficult to convey the scale of the undertaking embarked upon by policemen and women throughout the country in the hunt for Robert Black. In the Newcastle incident room alone 7 million one-line entries were studied by women officers viewing the microfiched AG30s. Once they had extracted as much information as possible about Black's fuel purchases in England and Scotland during the weekend that Susan

Maxwell had disappeared, the exercise had to be repeated for the days surrounding the abductions of Caroline Hogg and Sarah Harper, and the attempted abduction of Teresa Thornhill.

In the case of these three girls there was no question of forms AG30 being unavailable. The offences against all three had been committed during the previous seven years, so all petrol sale documentation had been retained in compliance with the VAT regulations. This information all had to be substantiated by follow-up inquiries. As an example, over fifty written statements were obtained to prove beyond reasonable doubt that Black had stopped for fuel at the Stannington service station on the A1 between Newcastle upon Tyne and Morpeth, between 11 a.m. and 1 p.m. on 30 July 1982. Multiplied fifty-fold, a conservative estimate of the number of refuelling stops Robert Black must have made during his critical journeys to Scotland, the north of England and the Midlands during the 1980s, and one gets some indication of the number of people who were interviewed, the statements that were obtained and the microfiched records that were checked and scrutinised.

Concomitant inquiries were being made of highway authorities regarding roadworks and diversions that had been in place on the material days, and also at many advertising companies to identify campaigns that had been current at the time of the abductions and murders attributed to Robert Black.

Detective Constable Lindsey (Les) McBride was one of the Lothian and Borders officers engaged in carrying out this side of the investigation. McBride had only become involved after Black's arrest at Stow, but since then had spent many days away from home liaising with detectives from other forces, and visiting advertising companies in an effort to trace those that had done business in previous years with Poster Dispatch and Storage.

Most of the companies identified still had copies of invoices, delivery notes and other documentation relating to their dealings with PDS; subsequent inquiries at that company by McBride and his colleagues to establish the dates and destinations of poster deliveries made by Black during the relevant periods were therefore reasonably straightforward. From the fuel and advertising information was deduced Black's probable route, and the likelihood or otherwise of his having been in the vicinity of the crimes at the material times.

The investigation was a classic example of effective inter-force co-operation. Most of the evidence gathered by the Staffordshire and Lothian and Borders detectives required verifying, a task that frequently entailed further inquiries and interviews across the country.

By December 1990, Hector Clark and his colleagues had decided that enough circumstantial evidence had been accumulated, and that there was now a reasonable prospect of obtaining a conviction against Robert Black. A decision to proceed with the prosecution lay not with the police but with the Crown Prosecution Service. Clark was aware that the CPS would be unlikely to sanction proceedings in such a potentially contentious case unless the scales were weighted in the prosecution's favour.

Clark judged that in the case of Black, success was certainly not a foregone conclusion. Although there was a wealth of circumstantial evidence pointing to Robert Black as the killer, the lack of direct or forensic evidence, together with evidence of identification that he knew would be strongly challenged by defence lawyers, could prove to be the prosecution's Achilles' heel. Clark and his colleagues believed that if Black confessed the case for the prosecution would be clinched. He had little to lose by owning up to the abductions and murders, as he was currently at the start of an indeterminate life sentence for the Stow abduction.

It was decided to conduct a second interview with Black and that it should take place in England. A team of detectives was assembled who would take it in turn to question Black, who this time would have his solicitor present. On the appointed day Robert Black was collected by car from HMP Peterhead on Scotland's north-eastern coast and driven the 200 miles to Alnwick police station in Northumberland, there to be questioned by the squad of detectives. This time there was no preamble: he was asked directly about crimes he was suspected of having committed. For three consecutive days, with breaks only for food, rest and exercise, the questioning continued. Black was obdurate; acting upon the advice of his solicitor he replied, 'No comment,' to every question put to him.

When eventually he was driven back to Peterhead he left behind him a frustrated and exhausted squad of detectives. There was to be no confession. The case against Robert Black was going to have to stand or fall on the evidence available.

CHAPTER 13

COUNTDOWN TO TRIAL

In preparing a case for eventual trial, Hector Clark and his colleagues were immediately faced with a fundamental problem. Of the offences on which it was hoped to proceed, only the abduction of Caroline Hogg could with certainty be said to have taken place in Scotland. It was possible that Caroline and Susan Maxwell had also been murdered north of the border, but this was by no means definite; an equally feasible hypothesis was that they had still been alive when Black crossed the border and came within English jurisdiction.

In view of this complication it was decided to await a decision by the Crown Office in Scotland on the Hogg abduction before proceeding further. Detective Superintendent Andrew Watt and Detective Chief Inspector Roger Orr were deputed to compile the report on Caroline Hogg's abduction. They completed this assignment expeditiously, and in accordance with Scottish procedural rules submitted it to Duncan Lowe, the local Procurator Fiscal for the Lothian and Borders region. After making a preliminary assessment of the report the Fiscal forwarded it to the Crown Office for consideration by counsel who would advise as to whether or not to proceed.

Clark was not surprised when after six weeks the report was returned with a decision not to proceed with a Hogg prosecution. In the absence of direct or forensic evidence or a confession, and taking into account the lapse in time which rendered identification evidence unreliable, it was not considered viable to go ahead. There being no objection by the Scottish Crown Office to the Hogg case being dealt with in England along with other matters of which Black was suspected relating to Susan Maxwell, Sarah Harper and Teresa Thornhill, Clark was instructed to prepare a comprehensive report for the Crown Prosecution Service, to be submitted through the Director of Public Prosecutions. This would considerably enlarge the scope of a prosecution case against Robert Black.

There were so many different facets to a case that involved four children and extended over eight years that Clark and his colleagues came to the conclusion that separate reports should be compiled detailing each offence and the local investigation that followed, together with supplementary reports covering the most important aspects of the overall inquiry. The entire package would be knitted together with an inclusive covering report prepared by Andrew Watt and Roger Orr for submission to the DPP.

The difference between Scottish and English jurisdiction continued to be a problem, initially to the police, later to the Crown Prosecution Service. The interviews conducted with Black following his conviction for the Stow abduction are one example. The first in Edinburgh had been carried out in accordance with strict Scottish rules; the other under equally rigorous, but procedurally different English ones. The question raised was whether details from the revealing Scottish questioning would be accepted by an English court, or whether that court would only be prepared to hear of the unproductive Alnwick interview.

Similarly with witness statements; the rules governing the taking of written testimony are materially different north and south of the border. This meant that people who had made statements under Scottish rules had to be seen again and their statements retaken in accordance with English procedure.

While these and other matters relating to evidence admissible in England were being considered, elsewhere senior detectives from the police forces involved in the inquiry were preparing detailed reports of their own force participation, and its contribution to the overall effort.

Andrew Watt and Roger Orr's task of writing the covering report was an awesome responsibility. Supplemented by the other reports from police forces in England and Scotland, it would have a considerable influence with the Director of Public Prosecutions and the Crown Prosecution Service in their decision-making. The attention to detail and objectivity of the reports making up the final package bore testimony to the tremendous efforts that over the years had gone into the inquiry.

The statistics alone were staggering; during the eight-year period that police had been investigating the cases, they had interviewed nearly 190,000 people and had obtained over 60,000 statements. Over 55,000 inquiries and initiatives had been carried out by police officers in England

and Scotland. To encapsulate this information into a coherent whole was itself a formidable undertaking requiring weeks of single-mindedness on the part of Andrew Watt and Roger Orr.

During the time this report was being prepared a development was taking place unbeknown to Hector Clark. When eventually it came to his knowledge it caused him considerable irritation and exasperation. Ray Wyre, the Director of the Gracewell Clinic at Birmingham, who had interviewed Robert Black and prepared a report at the time of his aborted appeal against his life sentence, was the object of Clark's rancour.

During the course of Wyre's interviews with Black at Saughton Prison prior to the appeal hearing, a bond had developed between the two men. According to Wyre this had been born of Black's desire to discover the source of his aberrant behaviour. Subsequently, at Robert Black's request, Ray Wyre visited him regularly from mid-November 1990 until the spring of 1993. During that time Black opened up to Wyre, describing his early life, detailing the offences of which he had been convicted and attempting to explain his innermost thoughts and the impulses that had driven him into committing assaults against children. Skilful questioning by Wyre in part succeeded in getting Black to question those desires and the urgings that had prompted his behaviour.

Wyre's objective, as at the Gracewell Clinic, was to persuade his client (Black) to face up to his deviancy. In over thirty hours of tape-recorded interviews Black revealed to Wyre many of his thoughts, most of which he had never divulged to the police. There was, however, one significant exception; although at times he came close to doing so, Black never admitted the abduction and murders of Susan Maxwell, Caroline Hogg or Sarah Harper. He had earlier spoken freely about the assaults of which he had been convicted in his youth, and of the attempted abduction of Teresa Thornhill at Nottingham, and of Mandy Wilson's abduction at Stow, but nothing Wyre said could induce him to go further.

Hector Clark first learnt of the interviews Wyre had had with Robert Black when partial transcripts of them appeared in several national newspapers in the days following Black's conviction. A Channel 4 programme on the day after the trial also transmitted extracts from the taped interviews interspersed by commentary by Ray Wyre. Hector Clark and John Stainthorpe's observations about the investigation were inserted into the programme, together with quotes from Elizabeth and Fordyce Maxwell and Jackie Harper and her mother.

Hector Clark's and his colleagues' sense of grievance at not having been made aware of Wyre's initiative is understandable. Nevertheless, neither the television programme, Ray Wyre's book detailing his interviews with Black nor the newspaper extracts appear to have revealed anything that would have been of direct assistance to the police in the task in which they were currently engaged of gathering evidence regarding the Maxwell, Hogg, Harper and Thornhill crimes. Many of Black's replies to Wyre's questions gave an insight into his thinking and motivation, and he seemed to be well informed about the disappearance of Genette Tate, the Devonshire girl who went missing while on her paper round in August 1978, apart from which there was little else.

On the other hand there appears to have been no valid reason why Wyre should not have provided police with transcripts of the tape-recorded interviews he was having with Robert Black. He was bound only by his own code of confidentiality, and was not to know what value Black's comments would have had for the police. The entire episode served only to illustrate the gulf that continues to exist between the police and the welfare and caring organisations.

By May 1991, the report for the Crown Prosecution Service was complete. It was a bulky package that Andrew Watt and Roger Orr took with them on 21 May 1993, as they drove down to London to deliver the report. Afterwards, as both men returned to Edinburgh, they were satisfied that everything possible had been done to bring to justice the man they believed was responsible for the child serial killings.

The matter was now out of their hands and beyond further influence. It was up to the lawyers of the Crown Prosecution Service to study the reports, consider the possibilities and probabilities, and examine carefully the key issues before eventually arriving at a considered and balanced judgement. In doing so they had to be objective, insensitive to any pressure from official sources, and uninfluenced by possible public reaction. Meanwhile Hector Clark and other policemen and women engaged in the Robert Black inquiry resumed their daily tasks pending a decision by the CPS.

Weeks extended into months with no word from the office of the Director of Public Prosecutions lying within the shadow of St Paul's Cathedral. Everyone was waiting for the decision: policemen, the victims' families, the media and politicians, all anxious to discover whether the man currently settling into a life of six-a-side football, table tennis and darts at Peterhead would have it interrupted to stand trial again.

Two months after Andrew Watt and Roger Orr had travelled down to

London came the first stirrings from the media. On 31 July 1991, Central Television announced that Robert Black was to be charged, a claim that was promptly refuted by Hector Clark.

Another seven months passed, a delay that prompted Merlyn Rees, a former Labour Home Secretary, to step in. At the end of February 1992, he wrote to the Attorney General asking him what was happening, and whether a decision had been made without it being made public. He expressed concern also on behalf of Jackie Harper. Coinciding with Merlyn Rees's request for information, Hector Clark announced that there were no further developments in the child murder investigation.

Responding to the growing demand for information, a spokesman for the Crown Prosecution Service announced: 'This is a complex case and we have a lot of material to review. It is under active consideration and a decision will be made as soon as possible.'

Soon after this announcement a decision was in fact made. On the evening of Wednesday, 11 March 1992, Hector Clark told a crowded news conference: 'Following a lengthy and complicated investigation by detectives here in Edinburgh and in five other UK police forces, I can confirm that criminal proceedings have been issued on the authority of the Crown Prosecution Service against Robert Black, aged forty-four, a van driver from London.'

To the policeman's chagrin the news had earlier been leaked to the media and an announcement on the 6 p.m. news had pre-empted Clark. No harm was done as he had already warned the victims' families that the news might break prematurely, but the early disclosure did nothing to enhance Clark's relationship with the media.

Nine days later the summonses were received at the Lothian and Borders Police headquarters at Fettes Avenue in Edinburgh, for service on Robert Black in Peterhead Prison. There were ten summonses in all (see Appendix).

Although the evidence was only circumstantial, most of the offences could be said to have been committed in England. In the case of Susan Maxwell and Caroline Hogg, either girl could have died while Black was in Scotland, although his avowed intention after his arrest at Stow of taking Mandy Wilson, his victim, to Blackpool to spend more time with her, suggested that his victims stayed alive for a longer, rather than a shorter period.

Twelve days later, on Wednesday, 1 April 1992, Andrew Watt and Roger Orr set off for Peterhead Prison to serve Black with the summonses Watt was carrying in his black official briefcase. The two men arrived at the bleak Victorian gaol perched on top of a hill overlooking the fishing port of the same name; after identifying themselves at the gate office, they were escorted across the prison yard to the main cell block. There, in a room used normally by lawyers, probation officers and other official visitors, they awaited Robert Black's arrival.

A few minutes later he entered the room wearing the regulation striped blue shirt and blue jeans. The meeting was brief; without further introduction, Watt explained to Black the reason for their visit before handing him the summons documents. Black made no comment until the policemen were about to leave the room. 'Tell Pamela she's not responsible for all this,' he said. Watt and Orr paused and Andrew Watt asked Black what he meant by the remark, but the other man fell silent, aware that he may already have said too much. When Hector Clark was told later of Black's comment, he agreed with the two detectives that it was significant; in the opinion of all three men it was a covert admission of guilt.

The summonses having been served on Robert Black it remained now for committal proceedings to go ahead. The preliminary hearings in the magistrates' court were to extend for nearly two years. The pattern was set at the magistrates' court hearing in July 1992 at which Robert Black's presence was not required. After a short hearing the case was adjourned for the first time.

The inordinate delay in bringing the case to trial stemmed mainly from the need to resolve several crucial matters at the lower court. The prosecution would stand or fall on the outcome of the pre-trial decisions reached.

Although there were to be changes before the trial opened, it was during this period that the lawyers who had been engaged to battle it out in the Crown Court were making their preliminary assessments, and planning their strategy. John Milford QC, a well-known and respected north-eastern advocate, was to lead for the prosecution assisted by Toby Hedworth and Roger Cooper. Herbert Kerrigan again represented Black during the preliminary hearings, with Alan Rawley QC appearing at a later stage. By the time the trial opened both men had retired from the scene and had been replaced by Ronald Thwaites QC, a London-based barrister, and his junior Mr William McCormick.

As the many complicated issues surrounding the trial gradually emerged, the time taken up by the CPS in deciding whether or not to go ahead with a prosecution became understandable. All were of vital importance, and although with regard to many, the final word would lie with the trial judge, the task the CPS lawyers had faced in weighing up the evidence before trusting that their decisions would later be endorsed by events, justified the prolonged and careful consideration they had been given.

There were three principal matters in contention. The first was jurisdiction; the Caroline Hogg abduction, with which the Scottish Crown Office had decided not to proceed, was the offence which could be said without doubt to have occurred in Scotland. It seemed likely that both she and Susan Maxwell had been killed in England. In view of the Scottish Crown Office's decision to allow the Hogg abduction to be considered along with the other offences by the Crown Prosecution Service, there was no real problem in deciding to go ahead with a prosecution in England.

The second issue was that of severance of the charges. The CPS lawyers had to prepare their arguments to counter an anticipated defence application to have the charges dealt with separately. If the judge ruled in favour of severance it would have a disastrous effect upon the prosecution, and would in all likelihood rule out their chances of success.

The third issue, that of linkage, was likely to prove the most contentious. In order to convince the jury that Robert Black was responsible for having committed all the offences with which he was charged, it would be incumbent upon the prosecution to demonstrate a similarity in the *modus operandi*, and other features common to them all.

The prosecution proposed to ask the judge to consent to the introduction of evidence relating to the Stow abduction of which Black had been convicted. Although unusual, this request was not without precedent; although details of previous convictions were not normally disclosed until after the current conviction, an earlier legal ruling had laid down that such information could be imparted to the jury earlier if it could be demonstrated that the facts of the earlier case(s) were so like those being tried, that the judge took the view that the probative effect of their being revealed far exceeded the prejudicial effect their admission would engender. These were matters that would have to be considered and ruled upon by the trial judge. In the meantime the prosecution would need to give them considerable thought, and prepare convincing arguments in their support.

A matter which affected the police was that of disclosure. This entailed the prosecution disclosing their case to the opposition, including witnesses' statements and exhibits, before the accused was committed for trial. No reciprocal arrangements existed, leading to criticism that proceedings were unfairly loaded in favour of the defence.

These arguments notwithstanding, there was a problem central to disclosure in the Black case: the amount of evidence accumulated since Susan Maxwell's abduction in July 1982. This evidence was not located in one place but was spread among six incident rooms and the Child Murder Bureau at Bradford. It mattered not that the Crown would not be introducing much of the material, it all had to be made available to the defence.

It was a complex logistical problem. Even had they been prepared to do so, the defence team could not reasonably be expected to visit locations in different parts of the United Kingdom. The answer lay in finding a suitable building convenient for the courts, at which all the prosecution material could be gathered and made available for examination. After much searching a five-storeyed office building at 90–92 Pilgrim Street, near the centre of Newcastle upon Tyne, was found. The first floor and the basement were entirely taken over by the inquiry teams and for several days following acquisition of the premises, police vehicles arrived from the various incident rooms in England and Scotland loaded with documents and other evidence. From Staffordshire a Pickfords removal pantechnicon deposited two tons of material at the Pilgrim Street office.

Every inch of space was utilised; in the basement of the building, set among a maze of central heating pipes, several dozen metal filing cabinets lined the bare-bricked walls. On the first floor metal shelves, specially assembled for the purpose, accommodated hundreds of box files, boxes of index cards and rows of official memorandum books. Part of the floor space was also stacked with large cardboard boxes containing exhibits.

A section of the office, with its three large windows looking out on Pilgrim Street, was taken up with five desks at which sat detectives drawn from the forces involved in the inquiry. Four computer consoles, three linked to the HOLMES system at Bradford, the other to the Lothian and Borders database at Edinburgh, sat on the desks. From the grey-painted walls pictures of Robert Black, Susan Maxwell, Caroline Hogg and Sarah Harper shared space with large wall maps of the United Kingdom on which different coloured pins indicated Black's destinations, the scenes of the abductions and the places where the bodies were found.

In charge of this complex was Detective Chief Inspector Roger Orr. Andrew Watt had recently moved to the Scottish Office, leaving the colleague with whom he had worked for so long to oversee the vital period leading up to the trial.

When everything had been deposited and sorted at Pilgrim Street, prosecution and defence lawyers took it in turn to visit. Their first sight of the vast amount of documentation and other material must have been a daunting experience, more so perhaps for the defence representatives who were given freedom to examine anything they wished. Despite having detectives available and willing to give every assistance, it was an impossible task to go through everything that was available for inspection.

Following the committal, prosecution and defence lawyers appeared before Mr Justice Macpherson at the Royal Courts of Justice in the Strand. Before a major trial it is not unusual for the trial judge to be asked to rule on questions of admissibility, to listen to pre-trial submissions by counsel and to make clear the position regarding various procedural matters. This enables both sides to be made aware of the parameters within which they will have to present their respective cases. It also makes economic sense; if the prosecution is relying upon contentious issues, it is better by far for the judge to make an admissibility ruling before the trial begins, rather than risk incurring unnecessary costs should it later be abandoned.

On 24 January 1994, at a different venue, Chelmsford Crown Court, Mr Justice Macpherson made the rulings that were vital to a successful prosecution. The initiative at the hearing was taken by Alan Rawley QC, who was then still leading counsel for the defence. Of the several submissions he made, two were of crucial importance to both sides. He asked first that the cases be heard separately. For the prosecution it was essential that the crimes be regarded as a linked series. If the judge came down in favour of the defence application, the prosecution would have separately had to depend solely on circumstantial evidence. As the Scottish Crown Office had already decided not to press ahead with the Hogg case due to the lack of evidence, the prospect of separate English prosecutions being successful was minimal. As events transpired, both of the critical rulings made by Mr Justice Macpherson favoured the prosecution.

In the second of these the defence asked for a ruling on the highly contentious issue of similar fact. Should the prosecution be allowed to lead on evidence relating to the abductions and murders of Susan Maxwell, Caroline Hogg and Sarah Harper, the attempted abduction of Teresa Thornhill, and, most controversially of all, with details of Black's recent conviction for the Stow abduction? The judge's ruling in favour of the prosecution included the caveat that there should be no reference to the life sentence that Black was currently serving. Finally, Mr Justice Macpherson informed Alan Rawley that he would rule on some of his other submissions at the trial. The decisions the judge made at Chelmsford constituted a significant setback for the defence who would have to draw up their strategy accordingly.

Pre-trial developments did not end at Chelmsford. In March, barely a month before the trial was listed for hearing at Newcastle Crown Court, Mr Rawley applied for it to be put back. He explained that the case in which he was currently appearing at Manchester was overrunning, and that unless the Black trial was delayed, he would be unable to appear. While understanding of the defence advocate's situation, Mr Justice Macpherson turned down his request. Soon afterwards Ronald Thwaites took over. He had three weeks to prepare for the trial.

Irrespective of whether they are engaged by the prosecution or the defence, initially barristers frequently take a different view of a case from other lawyers with whom they will be siding. While studying the brief each analyses the case and assesses its strengths and weaknesses until eventually they agree a joint strategy.

The defence lawyers having by this time reached agreement, Mr Rawley's withdrawal from the pending trial and his replacement by Ronald Thwaites placed Herbert Kerrigan in an unwelcome situation. While Alan Rawley had already made several admissions to the prosecution, a tactic jointly agreed upon with Mr Kerrigan, Mr Thwaites was opposed to these concessions and immediately reversed them. Within a short time Herbert Kerrigan also withdrew from the case, to be replaced by an Irishman, Mr McCormick.

These late changes were a setback for the defence. With only three weeks remaining to the trial, the prosecution case against Robert Black had to be reassessed and a new strategy evolved. Not an impossible task, but one now lacking input from Herbert Kerrigan who had been involved with Robert Black since soon after his arrest in 1990.

Meanwhile, without such distractions, the prosecution team were going ahead with their preparations. John Milford and Toby Hedworth would in the main be responsible for leading the prosecution case, examining and cross-examining witnesses while Roger Cooper, the third member of the team, who had been studying the intricacies of the petrol agency card system and other issues, would provide expert briefing for the other two.

By mid-April preparations were complete. Preliminary hearings had resolved early applications; witnesses had been warned when and where to attend; and the documentation and exhibits at Pilgrim Street were ready to be produced. One other assembly was to take place. On the eve of the trial Mr Justice Macpherson invited reporters and journalists from newspapers and television to meet him informally at the Moot Hall. It was here that the trial was to take place rather than in the modern purpose-built complex a few hundred yards distant.

The gathering was impressive; representatives from national and local newspapers mingled with those from television companies. They listened attentively as the mufti-clad judge laid down the guidelines which, if complied with, would, it was hoped, avoid misunderstandings. After he had finished speaking, Mr Justice Macpherson invited questions from his audience which he and his clerk, together with other officials who were present, answered clearly and unambiguously. As the reporters, journalists and other media personnel departed at the end of the briefing, it would have been surprising if any of them was under any illusion as to what was expected of them, and of the possible consequences should they exceed the generous parameters that the judge had laid down.

It was a unique and astute initiative by Mr Justice Macpherson, and its efficacy in ensuring media co-operation and compliance was apparent throughout the trial.

CHAPTER 14

THE TRIAL

The Preliminaries

The Moot Hall bustled with activity as it approached 10 a.m. on the morning of Wednesday, 13 April 1994. Counsel, gowned and bewigged, carrying ribbon-tied documents under their arm, mingled with policemen, witnesses, reporters and members of the public around the entrance to the oak-panelled court room on this, the opening day of what had already been heralded as 'the trial of the decade'.

Earlier on that sunny morning, with a cool breeze rippling in from the north-east, photographers and camera crews claiming vantage points in Castle Garth to record the arrival of Robert Black, paused to watch as several vans arrived from Pilgrim Street. Under the watchful eye of Detective Constable McClure 15 tons of documentary evidence and exhibits, packed into crates with 'Lothian and Borders Police' stencilled on the sides, were unloaded and carried through a side entrance into the building. Security was impressive; while uniformed police officers guarded the outside of the Moot Hall, others equipped with metal detectors checked everyone entering the building.

Black's arrival from Durham Prison had been swiftly and efficiently carried out. At 9.30 a.m. a white police minibus with darkened windows had swept past waiting press and television cameramen, through an iron gateway, and had drawn up outside a cream-painted door at the side of the courthouse. Cameras had focused on Black as he emerged from the vehicle, his head shrouded in a blanket and handcuffed to a detective, and was hustled through the door and down to a cell beneath the court room.

As the minutes ticked by, No. 1 Court filled up. The room was dominated by two features; the judge's bench and the dock with its waist-high wooden surround topped by metal spikes. There was a burst of activity when more than forty reporters representing newspapers and journals worldwide were admitted. Members of the public followed and soon occupied the available seats in the public gallery. There were two women present whom police ensured obtained a clear view of the proceedings: Jackie Harper and her mother Marlene Hopton sat next to one another exchanging an occasional word and watching the activity going on before them. Accompanying them was a West Yorkshire detective, charged with keeping a protective eye on the pair. Jackie Harper's elder daughter Claire also managed to secure places for herself and her boyfriend Andres where they could sit unnoticed holding hands.

Anticipation heightened when counsel entered the court. The opposing advocates took their seats in front and to each side of the dock facing the bench. John Tilman Milford QC leading for the Crown, and his opponent Ronald Thwaites QC were both in their late forties. Milford, a spruce, slightly built man, had been called to the Bar in 1969, and had taken silk twenty years later. With chambers in Newcastle he normally practised on the north-eastern circuit. Ronald Thwaites had been a barrister since 1970. A dark, sombre-looking man wearing horn-rimmed spectacles, he was nevertheless a more flamboyant lawyer than Milford. His chambers were in the Temple and he regularly appeared at the Old Bailey.

Toby Hedworth, a burly man whose red hair peeping out from beneath his wig made him instantly recognisable, was one of the two junior counsel for the prosecution. Alongside him was Roger Cooper, small, slim and dark-haired, the youngest member of the prosecution team. Ronald Thwaites was supported by William McCormick, a young, broadly accented Irishman.

Presiding over the trial would be the Honourable Mr Justice Macpherson of Cluny and Blairgowrie. The 27th Chief of the Macpherson clan, Sir William Macpherson was sixty-eight years old at the time of the trial. Called to the Bar in 1952, he became a QC in 1971, a Recorder of the Crown Court a year later, and was appointed a Judge of the High Court, Queen's Bench Division, in 1983.

For the following weeks the lawyers were to be engaged in verbal pugilism. Milford the boxer, deft, subtle and precise, against Thwaites the scrapper, direct, pugnacious, determined, each hoping that at the end of their encounter their arguments would have been persuasive enough to carry the day. Meanwhile on that first morning they held last-minute consultations with their instructing solicitors while waiting for the first round to commence.

At 10 a.m. precisely the court rose as, through a door at the side of the judicial bench, the mace bearer entered followed by the red-robed and ermine-clad judge. Next to him as he took his seat sat the High Sheriff of Northumberland, Barbara Lyndon Skeggs, accompanied by her chaplain. After a word with the judge, Ronald Bean the Clerk of the Court ordered that Robert Black be brought up into the dock. It was the moment everyone had been awaiting: Black's first public appearance since being sentenced to life imprisonment at Edinburgh High Court four years previously for kidnapping the little girl in Stow.

A hush descended as the sound of footsteps on the steps leading to the dock heralded the arrival of Robert Black and his escort. All eyes were on the accused man as he appeared in the dock accompanied by two prison officers. He did not look very impressive; although his beard and moustache were trimmed, the tight-fitting, light blue-grey suit he was wearing bore testimony to the weight he had put on since he had last worn it. At the request of the defence, the suit had been retrieved from the police, having not seen the light of day for four years. Any hope he may have had of appearing more presentable was therefore nullified.

To the disappointment of some of those present the start of the trial was to be delayed. The jury, although selected, had not yet been sworn, having previously been invited by the judge to dwell for a couple of days on their availability and willingness or otherwise to commit themselves to a hearing that could last for several weeks. In addition Mr Thwaites had a couple of submissions to make in the absence of the jury. First of all the ten charges had to be formally put to Black and his plea taken. One by one they were read out by Mr Bean and to each in turn the accused, in a noticeable Scottish accent, pleaded, 'Not guilty.'

When these matters had been dealt with and before the jury returned, Mr Justice Macpherson made some important rulings. While prohibiting publication of any photographs of Black in case they should prejudice his trial, he allowed the name of the village where Black had been arrested in 1990 to be revealed; hitherto, on the express order of Lord Ross, the earlier trial judge, its identity together with that of the six-year-old victim on that occasion had been kept from the press. Mr Justice Macpherson also strongly warned the media against disclosing the fact that Robert Black was currently serving a prison sentence.

Finally the six men and six women who were to comprise the jury were recalled. With innate courtesy Mr Justice Macpherson asked if any of them had a valid reason for being excused from jury service. There being no reply, each of them in turn was sworn in by the Clerk of the Court. At the end of the preliminaries, which had taken up most of the morning, the judge deemed it convenient to adjourn for lunch.

Prosecution

'May it please your lordship, members of the jury . . .' It was just after 2 p.m. when John Milford QC stood up to describe Robert Black's arrest in 1990 after the kidnapping and assault on the six-year-old girl at Stow. That offence was a 'carbon copy' of those of which he was accused. 'It is as if on this occasion Black was repeating almost exactly what had happened at Coldstream,' said Mr Milford.

The court listened as the prosecuting counsel described the circumstances surrounding the abduction and murder of Susan Maxwell. He described her as a bright, friendly but cautious child; a Girl Guide keen on tennis who owned a pony called Peanuts. John Milford then recalled the events of that summer afternoon twelve years previously as Susan was walking home after her game of tennis.

During her walk she had passed some children swimming in the river. Commenting on this Mr Milford said: 'It would be a place attractive to a man with an unhealthy interest in young girls, where he could find children on a hot day in a state of undress, a place likely to excite or arouse . . .' After crossing the Tweed bridge, 'Susan walked on, not many yards into England and then she disappeared as if into thin air.' Of Susan Maxwell's subsequent fate counsel said: 'The time of her death cannot be determined exactly, but we believe she was still alive on the journey. She was killed at or near the lay-by where she was dumped.'

Those in court were already getting a foretaste of the horrors to come. Ending his summary of the Susan Maxwell abduction, Mr Milford reminded the jury that 'For a child to be taken away and murdered is every parent's nightmare. It is perhaps easy, too easy, to dwell on all the suffering there must have been, of the children themselves and of those who loved them . . . We must consider without passion only the central issue. Is it proved by the evidence that it was this defendant, Robert Black, who abducted those little girls and killed them, and also abducted, albeit briefly, another girl in Nottingham, Teresa Thornhill?' Here Mr Milford paused to enable the jury to digest what he had said so far, before he moved on to the abduction of Caroline Hogg.

He said that Caroline had gone missing almost a year later, on another sweltering hot Friday in July 1983. The five-year-old had gone out to play for a few minutes after returning home from a party. Her decomposing remains were found ten days later on 18 July, 308 miles from Portobello near a lay-by on the A444 at Twycross in Leicestershire.

Explaining to the jury that Caroline lived with her mother and stepfather, Mr Milford went on, 'She had been to a party and was wearing a pretty dress and white ankle socks when she went down to the promenade. On that day Mr Black had set off in his Ford Transit van and he had been at Mills and Allen on the Portobello Road. Several witnesses describe seeing Caroline with a scruffy man.'

Throughout John Milford's opening address, Jackie Harper and her mother Marlene Hopton had sat tightly holding hands and sobbing quietly together as details emerged surrounding the fate of Susan Maxwell and Caroline Hogg. Their eyes remained fixed on the Crown prosecutor, avoiding Black who listened impassively from the dock. When Mr Milford moved on to Sarah Harper's abduction and murder, however, the two women had more difficulty in restraining their emotions, and sat hugging, sobbing and clenching their fists.

Sarah, the jury were told, disappeared sometime after 8 p.m. on Wednesday, 26 March 1986. It was a wet evening and she was wearing an anorak over a pink skirt and white socks. She had been to a corner shop a few yards away from home on an errand for her mother, and had vanished while returning. Her body had been found floating in the River Trent at Wilford, Nottingham, on Saturday, 19 April. 'It is no distance at all that the child had to walk, but again, as she walked down that street, she disappeared into thin air.'

Mr Milford went on to describe how a man out walking his dog had found Sarah's body floating in the River Trent. She had been violently attacked and then sexually assaulted. 'Sarah had been drowned,' Mr Milford stated. 'Her body bore a number of injuries consistent with abduction. Injuries to her head and neck suggest that she may have been unconscious when put in the water. Let us hope that is so,' he added quietly.

It was too much for Jackie Harper; sobbing bitterly she was led from the public gallery by her mother, and accompanied by the West Yorkshire detective. Black was unmoved by the interruption; his gaze remained on Mr Milford, waiting for him to continue.

The three murders had several features in common, claimed counsel.

Each of the victims was female, each of them had been taken from a public place, and in all three abductions a vehicle must have been in the vicinity to carry the child away. The motive for the abductions had been sexual; Susan Maxwell's pants had been removed, Caroline Hogg was found naked and Sarah Harper had sustained horrendous sexual injuries. After having been abducted they had each been taken south for a considerable distance following which, said Mr Milford, 'no serious attempt had been made to conceal the bodies. None had been buried, but none were left where they could immediately be found. Each of those young girls at the time of being abducted was bare-legged, save for white socks.'

He told the court that the locations at which the bodies had been found formed what detectives described as the 'Midlands Triangle'. Maps were produced to indicate to the judge and jury the area referred to; Mr Milford drew attention to Donisthorpe, the village where Black had regularly visited a son of the London family with whom he had been lodging.

The Crown advocate pointed out further similarities in the three cases. Susan Maxwell and Caroline Hogg were both abducted on a hot Friday in July. July and heat, Mr Milford submitted, were important themes in the case. Children had been bathing near the location of these abductions; in the case of Susan, in the river below the Tweed bridge, and in Caroline's case off the beach at Portobello. Furthermore, both bodies were found adjacent to a lay-by.

Referring to the similarities between the Susan Maxwell and Sarah Harper cases, Mr Milford said that a Transit-type van was associated with each abduction, and that although the victims had been partly undressed to facilitate sexual assaults, they had had their clothes put back on before being dumped.

In summarising the case against the accused, John Milford encapsulated the main points of the Crown case in one short statement: 'These three offences are so unusual, the points of similarity so numerous and peculiar that it is submitted to you that you can safely conclude that they were all the work of one man. The Crown alleges that Robert Black kidnapped each of his victims for sexual gratification, that he transported them far from the point of abduction and murdered them.'

Going on to describe the abduction of the six-year-old girl in a Borders village on 14 July 1990, Mr Milford told the jury how Black, who was bare-chested at the time, had snatched the child from the side of the main road that passed through the village and had driven to a lay-by where he had removed her shoes and socks.

'He had bound her hands behind her back, gagged her mouth with Elastoplast, placed a hood over her head and – to give you some sort of idea of the state of sexual excitement he must have been in, even in the short time he had had the child – he had indecently assaulted her. Then he had concealed her in his sleeping bag at the back of his van . . .'

Mr Milford paused to enable the events described to register themselves on the minds of the jury, before continuing: 'By good fortune he had been spotted by someone actually snatching the child and so it was that his vehicle was stopped and he was arrested.'

Pointing out the similarity between this case and that of Susan Maxwell he said: 'The little girl in Stow was wearing shorts when she was taken, was bare-legged and was wearing white socks. She was to be transported many miles south. Again it was the end of the week, it was July and it was hot. Stow and Coldstream are similar villages only 25 miles apart . . . Even more remarkably, like Susan Maxwell, the little girl was wearing yellow shorts . . . These two offences, side by side, are virtually carbon copies – as though Black was repeating almost exactly what had happened at Coldstream.'

Mr Milford ended the first day's hearing by reminding the jury of Robert Black's presence nearby when the three little girls were abducted: 'On 30 July 1982 he was on his way north to Edinburgh. If he took what was then the most direct route he would have taken the A697 through Coldstream and passed the very place Susan disappeared. On 8 July 1983, when Caroline Hogg went missing in Portobello, he was delivering posters nearby . . . On 26 March 1986, when Sarah Harper went missing, he was delivering posters about 150 yards away.'

As the court emptied many of those who had been present, reflecting upon what they had heard, would doubtless have had some misgivings about what future days had in store. Meanwhile Robert Black was heading back to Durham Prison.

On the day that Frederick West, a fifty-two-year-old builder, was charged in Gloucester with a tenth murder, that of his first wife, 260 miles away in Newcastle's Moot Hall, the trial of Robert Black was about to enter its second day. As John Milford prepared to resume, the press seats and the public gallery were again full. Deputy Chief Constable Hector Clark had taken his usual seat immediately behind the dock, within an arm's length of Black.

It was Black's counsel Ronald Thwaites who first stood up. He informed Mr Justice Macpherson that he had a submission to make with the jury absent. After the jury had filed out, Mr Thwaites requested that he be allowed to make his opening speech immediately following that of John Milford, instead of at the end of the prosecution as was usual. He submitted that in such a complicated case it would be useful if the jury had advance notification of matters likely to be contested by the defence. After pondering over the matter, Mr Justice Macpherson turned down Ronald Thwaites' request, stating that on the only previous occasion on which he had allowed such a course, he had later been severely criticised.

After the jury had re-entered court John Milford continued with his opening address. He moved on from the murders to April 1988 and the attempted abduction of Teresa Thornhill. It was about 7.30 p.m. on Sunday, 24 April 1988, Mr Milford told the jury. Fifteen-year-old Teresa, wearing a pink skirt and blouse, was walking home with her boyfriend Andrew Beeston when a dark blue Transit van passed them and turned right into Norton Street. The couple parted company and Teresa followed the direction the van had taken into Norton Street. It had stopped on the opposite side of the road, and the driver was out of the vehicle which had its bonnet raised. 'He tried to attract her attention by asking her if she could fix engines, whereupon she was grabbed in a bear-hug and a determined attempt was made to put her by force into the van . . .'

The Crown advocate said that Teresa looked considerably younger than her fifteen years, and was similar in appearance to the other three girls. This age advantage had enabled her to put up a spirited resistance; fortunately also, Andrew Beeston had seen what was taking place and had run to her assistance. As a result, said Mr Milford, 'The abductor realised that he was not going to get away with it so he sped off in his vehicle . . .'

Teresa, although greatly distressed by the incident, was nevertheless able to furnish police with a description of her assailant, one that fitted Black. He was aged between thirty and forty, 5 ft 6 ins to 5 ft 8 ins tall, heavily built with a big stomach, bald, unshaven and with a moustache. In addition he was wearing dark glasses and he smelled. Mr Milford observed, 'as far as smelling, he was known by some of the sons of the Rayson family as "Smelly Bob".' As Mr Milford spoke these words some members of the jury looked across at Black who remained impassive, while his escort stared stonily ahead.

At this point Mr Milford digressed to tell the court something of Black's employment record. He had come down from Scotland to London in 1968 and had taken casual work for several years until in 1976 he obtained regular employment as a van driver delivering posters throughout England and Scotland. Mr Milford told the jury how Black's employers had provided him with a credit card which had enabled him to purchase fuel; every transaction, including the date, time and place, had been logged at the petroleum company's headquarters, and it was by painstakingly checking these records, many of which dated back to 1982, together with records of his deliveries, that detectives had been able to trace his route on the relevant days. This further enabled them to establish where he had been delivering the posters, which in turn showed him to be in the vicinity of the abductions.

Mr Milford said that prior to the attack on Teresa Thornhill in Nottingham, Black had been to a number of places in the north of England. The day after the attack he was back in London, and by 27 April had returned to Nottingham. Referring again to the Nottingham attack, Mr Milford pointed out that although it had proved abortive, 'we have Mr Black's hallmarks – a female child abducted in a public place into a vehicle and, you may think, for only one reason, a sexual motive'. He continued: 'We have here a series of offences, Maxwell in July 1982, Hogg in July 1983, Harper in March 1986, Thornhill in April 1988 and the little girl in the Borders in July 1990. It was beyond the realm of coincidence that one person could have been in all these places at these times.'

When John Milford sat down at the end of the second morning he had been outlining the prosecution case for over five hours. In the afternoon he was to call the first of his witnesses.

The early part of Thursday afternoon was taken up with reading out statements relating to Susan Maxwell made by witnesses including Elizabeth Maxwell, Susan's mother and Arthur Meadows, the lorry driver who had found her body, who the defence agreed need not be personally in attendance. Elizabeth Maxwell said that the day of her daughter's abduction was the first occasion on which she had been allowed to walk home alone. Her statement went on to tell of her subsequent decision to collect Susan from the tennis club rather than let her walk home, and her failing to meet her either on the way to the club or later. 'I telephoned relations where Susan might have gone,' she said, 'and at 5.30 p.m. my husband telephoned the police.'

Mrs Maxwell said that Susan was a cautious and obedient child, a view shared by Theresa O'Connor, the girl's form teacher at Berwick Middle School. Thoughtful, aware and unlikely to have got into a stranger's car, was her teacher's opinion. Her statement went on to say that Susan had got on well with her classmates, 'But while she was enthusiastic in all her school life, it was not the most important thing. Her home life was very important to her . . . Her manner was open and friendly but she kept an appropriate distance . . . I can't imagine her getting voluntarily into a car,' it concluded. A clear picture had emerged of a girl, well brought up, happy and obedient at both home and school, but who was also sensible, one who it was inconceivable would have voluntarily entered a stranger's vehicle.

Testifying from the witness box, Dr Scholz van der Merwe, the pathologist who had examined Susan Maxwell's body at the place where it had been found, told the jury that his two-hour on-site examination had failed to reveal the exact cause of her death. Describing the harrowing scene that greeted him that morning, Dr van der Merwe said that the child's badly decomposed body was lying in woodland with police and forensic scientists already in attendance. She was wearing shorts and a yellow top, but no shoes. Her clothing appeared undisturbed, although he noticed that her head was resting on her folded pants.

Further details of a significant sighting made on the day of Susan Maxwell's abduction by a former Northumbrian policeman emerged during his cross-examination. Earlier Peter Currie, who had been medically retired from the force, and who now admitted to having a poor memory, had stated that between 3.50 p.m. and 4.10 p.m. on the day in question, he and his late wife had been driving towards Cornhill when they had passed a dirty white or cream-coloured Transit-type van which was stationary outside the gates of The Hirsel, the estate of Lord Home. The witness told Mr Thwaites that the vehicle had double doors, and that the back windows were covered in curtain material.

The jury had been told of Black's attack on the little girl at Stow during Mr Milford's opening speech; now they were to hear more from a short exchange between Mr Thwaites and Peter Currie during his cross-examination. After the witness had said that he had heard of Black's arrest on 14 July 1990, Mr Thwaites asked him: 'Did you hear of his court appearance in Edinburgh on 10 August 1990 when his case was disposed of?'

'I heard he had been to court.'

'Did any police officer visit you or your wife between his arrest and his conviction?'

'I was visited at about that time, or it may have been after.'

It was the similarities between the Stow abduction and those of Susan

Maxwell, Caroline Hogg and Sarah Harper that had immediately focused police attention on Black, and started the count-down procedure that ended in his standing accused of those offences.

Friday, 15 April, the third day of the trial and the final sitting before the weekend adjournment, was to see a succession of witnesses testifying. As on previous days a queue of people were waiting to be admitted and the usual army of newspaper and other media representatives were present to report the day's proceedings or any human interest item they thought worth reporting. Jackie Harper's return to the Moot Hall following her sudden departure on the first day was soon noticed. Accompanied by her mother and her detective escort, she took a seat in the public gallery from where she could see the dock.

James Fraser, a forensic scientist, told the jury that following Black's arrest in 1990 for the abduction and sexual assault on the six-year-old girl at Stow, more than 300 items that were later removed from his London lodgings and from his van were forensically examined. He said that he was one of a small team of scientists who had worked almost exclusively on the case for six months after the arrest. They had been provided with hair and body samples from Black, and had had access to 'almost all his worldly goods'.

Mr Thwaites elicited during his cross-examination that despite these efforts nothing of significant evidential value had been discovered. Asked if, after Black's arrest, he had been given a specific brief to establish a link between the defendant and any of the murdered girls, Fraser replied, 'Broadly speaking, yes.'

'Broadly speaking,' echoed Mr Thwaites, 'have you been able to make a scientific link between this man' – here he pointed at Black – 'and any of those murders?'

'No,' the witness replied.

Fraser went on to agree that in over 1800 microscopic comparisons, not a single match had been made. By establishing early on that there was nothing forensically to connect Black with the murders, the defence advocate had made an effective point.

However, in reply to John Milford's brief re-examination, the scientist went some way towards negating the defence argument by stating that the interval between the offences taking place and Black's arrest made it unlikely that anything significant would be discovered by forensic examination.

Dr Norman Weston, another forensic scientist, added little to his colleague's testimony. Weston had discovered a 'foreign hair' on the outside of Susan Maxwell's pants, but he reaffirmed what Fraser had said, that the time that had elapsed between the commission of the crime and his examination of the specimen had made it impossible to reach a definite conclusion.

When asked by Ronald Thwaites how closely the hair had matched samples from an earlier suspect in 1986, the witness replied cryptically, 'I was given to understand that this particular person was a good suspect and worth looking at.'

It had been an absorbing session, not least because it had made clear to the jury that the prosecution had little to offer in the way of forensic evidence to connect Robert Black with the crimes of which he was accused. As the court rose to adjourn for lunch, for the first time Black glanced towards the public gallery where he met the fixed stare of Jackie Harper. In an instant he looked away before disappearing downstairs.

The memory of the day twelve years earlier when Susan Maxwell had disappeared was printed indelibly on the mind of Raymond Wooding, a businessman from Ripon. One of the last people to see her alive, Wooding had parked his car and was standing on the Tweed bridge preparing for an evening's fishing, when he noticed a young girl walking on the opposite side of the road.

'She was carrying something,' he told the jury. 'I thought at first it was a fishing net, but when she got closer I could see it was a tennis racket. She was very distinctive. She was dressed very smartly in pale yellow.'

'Do you remember that day clearly?' Mr Milford asked him.

'It haunts me still,' the witness replied.

Another person who had seen Susan Maxwell walking home that afternoon was Karen Young, fifteen at the time and living in Coldstream. She said that she had been travelling with her grandparents in their car when she had spotted Susan walking over the Tweed bridge. 'I knew Susan and her family and thought it was very unusual for her to be walking home alone. It was not something she would do.'

The final witness on Friday was Eric Mould, a former director of Poster Dispatch and Storage, and Black's one-time employer. He told John Milford that Robert Black had joined the firm in 1978, and that it soon became apparent that he had a personal hygiene problem. He was scruffy in appearance, had dirty hair, rotten teeth and a problem with body odour.

'To put it bluntly, do you mean he smelled?' asked Mr Milford.

'Yes,' Mould replied. He went on to say that Black, although in receipt of an allowance, kept a sleeping bag and blanket in his van, and like other drivers on long runs slept in the vehicle. Black remained inscrutable and showed no reaction while his erstwhile employer testified.

After a weekend during which media attention had focused on the accidental shooting down over the northern Iraq no-fly zone of a United States helicopter by its own fighters, and at home on teenagers in council care who had gone on the rampage during a supervised day trip to a National Park beauty spot in Northumbria, the jury, themselves in the news, returned on Monday for their second week at the Moot Hall.

Robert Black's former boss and a succession of his ex-workmates were due to give evidence on Monday. Before he started to call them John Milford read out the statement of Arthur Meadows, the lorry driver who had discovered Susan Maxwell's body. Listening to the Crown advocate recalling that distant day, those in court, with the exception of the accused, could share the horror felt by Arthur Meadows upon coming across the decomposing body. 'I was frozen with fear,' he said. 'I turned and ran . . . I was still shaking when I reached the house.'

There was a palpable relaxing of the tension as Mr Milford finished reading and turned to call the day's first witness. Raymond Baker had been Black's boss at Poster Dispatch and Storage and told the jury that he had considered 'Robbie' to be a friend before he had been arrested in 1990 for the Stow abduction. After corroborating the testimony of his colleague Eric Mould, Baker went on to deny a defence suggestion that he was making 'exotic additions' to an earlier statement following visits from the police. He repeated his earlier observation that 'the only person who used curtains in the back of the van was Robert Black. They weren't fitted, just hung over the back doors.' It was becoming apparent that oblique attacks on the police, and attempts to cast doubt on the veracity of some of the prosecution witnesses, were to be an important aspect of the defence team's strategy.

Derek Wilcox, another PDS driver, told of his instant dismissal after having refused to do the Scottish run in July 1982. Black had agreed to do the deliveries in his place. The following day Susan Maxwell disappeared.

The next day was mainly taken up with evidence relating to the lengthy and painstaking inquiries made to track Black's movements around the country. Mr Milford told the jury that Black had been provided with an agency card that enabled him to purchase fuel. He explained how police had found out which petrol stations Black had used on his journeyings, and how they had succeeded in tracing other motorists who had used those filling stations on the same days as Black; those drivers had been asked to try and recall the time at which they had bought their fuel. By examining records it had then been possible to establish within a fairly short period the times that Black had made his fuel stops.

Thomas Cusack had known Robert Black since he had joined PDS in 1978. Initially he had been responsible for training him, a job that among other things entailed showing him the various routes and destinations served by the company. They had become friendly and on several occasions he had invited Black to his home. Later Black had adopted the habit of using different routes to other drivers. Mr Milford pointed out an unexplained gap between a refuelling stop Black had made at Carlisle and another at the Watford Gap on 31 July/1 August 1982. 'Would it have taken you more than twenty-four hours to get from Carlisle to the Watford Gap?' Mr Milford asked. 'No, definitely not,' replied Cusack.

Mr Thwaites' cross-examination concentrated at first on the impression of Black held by the witness and other PDS drivers. He asked the witness whether Black was 'considered a Walter Mitty, a bit of a bore in fact, because people always found him enthusing over A and B roads?' 'That's correct, yes,' Cusack replied.

The witness recalled that when Black had first joined PDS he had worn his hair in a 'Bobby Charlton' style so as to conceal his baldness. This had led to some teasing by his workmates. He had also worn glasses. By the 1980s he had abandoned both the hair style and the glasses; he no longer had any compunction about revealing his bald pate, and had taken to wearing contact lenses. Cusack agreed with counsel that by so doing he had become 'a completely different character'.

With a hand characteristically outstretched, Ronald Thwaites asked Cusack if, as had been stated, Black had refuelled at Stannington filling station, he could subsequently have made deliveries at Edinburgh, Dunfermline and Dundee, and still have arrived at Glasgow before 5 p.m. It was possible, agreed Cusack, providing Black had left Stannington by 10.30 a.m.

These times were to be disputed by the prosecution. While the defence maintained that records kept by the Glasgow poster recipients suggested that Black had delivered them before 5 p.m. Mr Milford introduced contrary evidence arguing that Black had not even reached Dundee until later that evening.

The matter was critical; if the jury accepted the defence contention it followed that it would have been impossible for Black to have been at Coldstream close to 4 p.m. on 30 July 1982, made deliveries at Edinburgh, Dunfermline and Dundee, and reached Glasgow before 5 p.m. However, if they decided that Black had not reached Dundee until later that evening, he could quite possibly have been in Coldstream at roughly the time that Susan Maxwell had disappeared. It may have occurred to the jury that if the prosecution was right, Susan may well have been in the back of Robert Black's Transit van when it arrived in Glasgow. As the court adjourned at the end of the fifth day, it was another small matter for them to dwell upon.

The proceedings so far had largely concentrated on the abduction and killing of Susan Maxwell. On day six the emphasis was to switch to Caroline Hogg. The five-year-old girl had last been seen on the Portobello promenade almost a year after Susan Maxwell had disappeared. Despite the vast amount of police time and resources devoted to the Maxwell case, to say nothing of the public's contribution, little solid progress had been made towards finding her killer.

It was shortly after the Caroline Hogg abduction that the decision had been made to link her inquiry with that of Susan Maxwell, with Hector Clark in overall command. It had been a logical move but despite the co-ordinated efforts of four police forces, aided now by the introduction of computerised equipment, both cases still remained unsolved. Now eleven years later, the jury were to hear of the events on that summer evening in 1983 when a little girl wearing party clothes had gone out to play, never to return. First, however, there was to be further testimony relating to the poster deliveries made by Black on the day that Susan Maxwell disappeared.

As has been pointed out, the delivery time at the Mills and Allen depot in Glasgow was critical. If Black had arrived there before 5 p.m. he would have been in the clear, as it would have been impossible for him to have been in the vicinity of Coldstream at 4 p.m., made his intermediate deliveries and still have arrived in Glasgow before five o'clock.

When police examined the Mills and Allen poster record book they had noticed something unusual. For several years past the entries had been made in the same handwriting. Upon checking further they discovered that two books were in existence, one used on a daily basis in which entries were made by different people, and the book they were already studying into which all entries had regularly been transferred by one person.

The man who should have accepted Black's delivery on 30 July had been on holiday. Deputising for him that day had been Hugh Crystal, and he it was who entered the witness box on the sixth day of the trial. He admitted that he showed the date on the invoice accompanying the posters as the actual date of their delivery, often resulting in dates and times being materially inaccurate.

Hugh Crystal monosyllabically affirmed every question put to him by Mr Milford. During cross-examination Mr Thwaites accused him of being incompetent, a slur which he appeared to particularly resent. Thenceforth he seemed determined not to cede any ground during questioning. Eventually Ronald Thwaites pointedly asked him who had told him of the importance of his evidence. Crystal's reply was unequivocal: 'I know it's important and you do, otherwise I wouldn't be standing here now would I?'

It was then the turn of Toby Hedworth, junior counsel for the prosecution, to read out statements recalling the evening of Caroline Hogg's abduction. A commanding figure showing a glimpse of red hair beneath his wig, Mr Hedworth first read out Annette Hogg's statement made two days after her daughter had vanished: 'Caroline is not allowed to go to the beach, the local park, the funfair or the amusement arcades. It was really drummed into her not to go to these places. She has been smacked for going to the park . . . I only let her play in the school playground or the housing estate behind our house where there was no traffic.'

Caroline had been to a friend's birthday party during the afternoon of her disappearance and 'on the way home she was full of fun . . .' Later she had asked her mother if she could go out to play. 'I said it was too late. Her dad then said she could go out if she changed her shoes, but only for five minutes and no further than the garden gate.' Caroline had only partly complied with those instructions, changing from her party shoes into a pair of pink trainers.

When her daughter had not returned after three-quarters of an hour, Mrs Hogg went outside to fetch her. 'I went to the front of the house and shouted her name out, but there was no reply. I looked out the back but there was no sign of her. I saw Stuart [Caroline's eleven-year-old brother] playing football outside but he had not seen her. John [Annette's husband] went down to the promenade and shouted for her, but there was no reply.'

Annette Hogg and other members of the family had then searched the area including the funfair, some nearby school playing fields where children had been seen, the promenade and the beach, all without finding any trace of the little five-year-old. Finally at 8.30 p.m. they had called the police.

Black sat still, his face expressionless while Toby Hedworth was speaking..Only after the barrister had finished did the man in the dock glance around the court. Two or three members of the jury looked in his direction while the rest of them watched Mr Hedworth as he had a word with John Milford before he prepared to read out the statement of Caroline's stepfather.

After describing Caroline as a happy and outgoing child, John Hogg's statement continued: 'She had been forbidden to go to the park. I don't think she would go with strangers as she had been warned about bad men and had seen a video at school about going with strangers. I persistently warned her about going to the promenade on her own. I can only think that she was enticed by someone who was able to gain her trust.'

As with Mrs Maxwell, the statements of Annette and John Hogg were accepted by the defence, saving them from the ordeal of attending court to testify personally.

On Thursday Mr Milford resumed calling his witnesses. The first one was Laura McPherson, a seventeen-year-old Tower Amusement arcade cashier, who said that on the day Caroline Hogg vanished she had been sitting on the sea wall at Portobello and had noticed the little girl on her own nearby. About twenty minutes later she again saw her, this time in company with a scruffy-looking man. The witness said that later that evening she had joined in the search for the missing girl.

Miss McPherson stated that about a fortnight later she was working in the arcade paybox when she had again seen the scruffy man whom she had seen on the previous occasion with Caroline. This time when he had left the arcade she had followed him along the promenade towards Fun City, but had lost him in the crowd. Later the same man reappeared in the arcade; she immediately alerted Mr Morrison her boss, who had gone after him but had also lost sight of him. They had straightaway informed the police, but by the time they arrived the man had gone.

Derek Jackson said that at the time Caroline went missing he was an attendant on the children's roundabout at Portobello's Fun City fairground. He knew Caroline Hogg and on that particular evening had seen her arrive at the fairground holding a man's hand. The witness told Mr Milford that the little girl had had a two-minute ride on a double-decker bus on his roundabout. 'The man with her paid me the 15p for the ride and just stood at the side.' Caroline and the stranger then left the amusement park, still holding hands.

Jackson went on to describe the man as stockily built, dirty-looking, with matted hair and about two days' growth of beard. He believed that he had been wearing spectacles. He later helped a police artist draw a likeness of a man closely resembling Robert Black. Neither Laura McPherson nor Derek Jackson was cross-examined.

It no doubt occurred to many of those in court that on the various occasions that the scruffy-looking man was spotted at or near the amusement park, an opportunity was missed. If it had indeed been Robert Black and he had been apprehended in that summer of 1983, and charged with the offences against Susan Maxwell and possibly also against Caroline Hogg, at least two other assaults might have been averted, and a child's life spared. No blame could be attributed to either witness as neither could have foreseen the subsequent events after they had spotted Caroline Hogg in the company of the stranger. Also, when later Laura McPherson and her boss followed Black, it is easy to understand how they lost sight of him amid the crowds thronging the promenade on that sunny evening at the seaside.

The seventh day's hearing ended on a harrowing note when Toby Hedworth read out the statement of Gary Roberts, the businessman who had discovered Caroline's body at the secluded Leicestershire lay-by. Roberts had stopped there 'to answer a call of nature', and as he descended into a ditch he had seen the naked body of a child lying in the bottom. He had run to a nearby cottage and from there had telephoned the police. The spectators and jury were particularly subdued as they left the court.

Friday, 22 April was the eighth day of the trial. With the story moving forward three years to the evening of 26 March 1986, it was to be no less dramatic than the previous days. Mr Hedworth opened the proceedings by telling the court that ten-year-old Sarah Harper, who lived in Morley, Leeds, had put on her anorak on what had been a rainswept evening before hurrying out from her home in Brunswick Place to buy a loaf and two packets of crisps at K & M Stores, a corner shop two minutes' walk away in Peel Street. Although she was seen returning home by several people, she never arrived. Her body was recovered twenty-four days later from the River Trent near Nottingham.

Counsel then read aloud her mother's statement in which she recalled that distant evening. It had been ten minutes to eight when Jackie Harper had asked her daughter to run to the corner shop for a loaf of bread. 'Sarah was happy to go,' she said. 'She asked Claire if she wanted to go with her, but she was still eating her tea. Normally they would go together when it was dark.'

Eight years later Claire Harper still clearly remembers the evening. In a recent interview she said: 'I know Sarah wanted me to go and buy some sweets with her. If only I'd been there too, it might never have happened . . .' Now, at the trial, Claire and her boyfriend Andres sat listening intently from the public seats.

When Sarah failed to arrive back home, Mrs Harper had twice sent her sister to look for her. She then went out herself but could find no sign of her daughter, although Mrs Champaneri, wife of the shop proprietor, remembered serving her. It was then that Jackie Harper informed the police about her missing daughter.

Later on Friday Mrs Harper made her third appearance at the trial, arriving in time for the afternoon session. With her detective escort she sat in the public gallery from where for the first time since the trial began she could study Black's face. At the same time she listened as witnesses told of having seen an unidentified man at different locations on the evening her daughter had disappeared.

Kevin Monaghan had seen a man who he thought resembled Peter Sutcliffe, the Yorkshire Ripper. 'He had black hair and quite a big beard. He just seemed to be loitering . . . looking a bit suspicious.'

George Bailey recalled a little girl wearing an anorak following him as he went to the corner shop. Inside the shop he had noticed a man who he thought was behaving suspiciously by lingering at a jar of sweets, while Nicola Gregson, who was a thirteen-year-old schoolgirl at the time, remembered seeing Sarah at about ten minutes to eight walking towards her home carrying a loaf of bread.

There had also been two significant sightings of a white Transit van that evening. Lesley Appleyard said that she had noticed a stranger getting into one near the Miner's Arms public house in Morley between half-past seven and a quarter to eight, while John Garlick who had been driving in pouring rain along the B6540 near Nottingham between 9.10 p.m. and 9.15 p.m. stated that he had seen a white Transit parked in a gateway with a bare-headed man standing by the passenger door. When he later read of Sarah Harper's disappearance he had contacted the police.

To validate Garlick's sighting, Police Sergeant Paul Cook said that in

September 1990, he had driven a Transit van from Sarah's home to the gateway, 82 miles of mainly motorway driving, in an hour and fifteen minutes. He stated that he had left Sarah Harper's address at 8 p.m. and had driven at between 70 and 80 m.p.h.

Both Garlick's and Sergeant Cook's testimony was challenged by the defence. After John Garlick had reaffirmed to Mr Thwaites that he had reported his sighting of the van after reading of Sarah Harper's disappearance, he denied defending counsel's suggestion that he had been influenced by anyone before coming to court. Mr Thwaites, in referring to a statement the witness had made in 1986 in which he had said that he did not recall any lettering on the van, demanded to know how he could now apparently improve his evidence by testifying that it had been definitely unmarked? Unruffled, Garlick merely repeated that it had been a plain van.

Sergeant Cook told Black's advocate that his journey had been made at a time that coincided with Sarah Harper's abduction some time after 8 p.m. and John Garlick's sighting of the van. He did not deny that police had wanted to see if such a journey was possible.

Mr Thwaites put it to the policeman that he had been racing to Nottingham, possibly at speeds of 85 m.p.h., to see if it could be done in time. 'You were never keeping to the speed limit, were you?' 'Yes, sir,' replied Cook. Referring to the police sergeant's claim that he had been driving at between 70 m.p.h. and 80 m.p.h. Mr Thwaites asked: 'You wouldn't have driven at those speeds in a Transit van if it had been pouring down?' 'Perhaps not,' Cook conceded. The exchanges between counsel and witnesses enlivened even more what had already been an absorbing day.

With the hearing adjourned until Monday, newspaper reports were temporarily given over to other news. In New York ex-President Nixon had lapsed into a coma, while nearer home, French preparations for the approaching D-day commemorations were going ahead. Other news items were depressingly familiar. The IRA murdered two people in Londonderry, and an eighty-five-year-old spinster died in hospital after being mugged by twelve-year-olds. On a lighter note, allegations of cheating at a golf match were read by readers bemused that such a matter could only be settled and pride restored by recourse to Nottingham County Court.

If any of those attending the trial had banished details of what they had heard to the backs of their minds during the weekend, on Monday matters were brought sharply back into focus. Professor John Jones, the Home Office pathologist who had carried out a post-mortem examination on Sarah Harper, estimated that she had died between five and eight hours after her last meal. He went on to tell the court that marks on her face suggested that she had been gagged before being subjected to such a savage attack that it had left her with 'very terrible injuries'. The injuries were consistent with her having been raped, although they could have been inflicted with some type of instrument, said Professor Jones.

'Further examination indicated the injuries had occurred during life,' said the pathologist, adding, 'The child was still alive at the time these injuries were inflicted.' His examination had revealed that Sarah's assailant had struck her also on the head, or banged it against an object. 'It's possible those injuries would have been sufficient to have stunned her . . . she might even have been unconscious,' concluded the witness.

Those in court listening to the pathologist's evidence were stunned by his harrowing testimony. In a voice in which he had been careful to conceal any emotion, Professor Jones had drawn a vivid picture of the agonising nightmare that must have enveloped the ten-year-old, culminating in her being dumped while still alive in the icy water of the River Soar. Several members of the jury looked across at the dock, but Robert Black remained impassive.

The shock of finding Sarah Harper's body, twenty-five days after she had disappeared, had fallen on thirty-seven-year-old David Moult who lived in the village of Wilford, near Nottingham. Before he started to give evidence a video film was shown in court of the footpath leading down to the River Trent near the spot where it was alleged Sarah's body was deposited in the river. The witness who had been out walking his dog Ben at the time, told the court: 'I was walking along the bank when I spotted something floating in the river. I thought it was just a piece of sacking then the current turned it round and I realised it was a body.' When it had travelled a little further downstream, Moult had been able with some difficulty to pull the object partly to the bank. 'I could see then that it was the body of a young person with fair, collar-length hair and a maroon-coloured top.'

Not once did she glance in the direction of the man sitting a few feet away in the dock. It was the tenth day of the trial and the slightly built figure of Teresa Ann Thornhill was testifying about the events that had occurred almost exactly six years earlier. As usual the court was packed with members of the public and other observers, while reporters recorded the words of the only victim to have survived among those named in the charges.

Teresa Thornhill told John Milford that on Sunday, 24 April 1988, she had been on the way home after a walk in the park with her boyfriend Andrew Beeston, and other friends. Soon after leaving Andrew she had noticed a van parked on the opposite side of the road.

'A man got out and opened the bonnet and asked, "Can you fix vans' engines?" I said no, and started walking faster. The next minute this guy came along and got me in a bear-hug.' Here the witness paused and demonstrated to the court the manner in which her attacker's arms had enveloped her. She continued: 'He lifted me off the ground and I was kicking my feet. At this stage I couldn't move because his arms were strong and I was so small. I was ready to pass out as his hand was so big I could hardly breathe. I then grabbed his arm and bit him on the forearm. I grabbed his testicles and he freed my arms.'

Teresa Thornhill had managed to knock off her assailant's glasses before he had got her to the van and attempted to force her inside. It was at this point that Andrew Beeston, having heard the commotion, had intervened. Only then did the man release his victim and drive off in his van.

In reply to Mr Milford, Miss Thornhill described her attacker as balding with grey hair around the sides, and with a beer belly. Her graphic description of her terrifying encounter had the court admiring her determination and ultimately successful struggle.

Mr Thwaites slowly stood up. Teresa Thornhill's unequivocal testimony persuaded the defending advocate to concentrate his cross-examination not so much on the circumstances surrounding the assault, but on more peripheral matters. Reverting to an earlier tactic, he questioned her about the apparent discrepancy between her earlier statements to the police in which no mention was made of white socks, and her testimony in court when she said that she had been wearing white socks at the time she was attacked. Had she not agreed to sell her story to the *Daily Mirror* after the trial, inquired Mr Thwaites, and had she not changed her evidence for the trial so as to give credence to the newspaper's evocative headline: MURDERED IN THEIR WHITE SOCKS? While agreeing that she had made arrangements to sell her story to the *Mirror*, the witness denied that she had been influenced into embellishing her evidence by the headline.

With arm outstretched, Ronald Thwaites then asked the witness why she had failed also to mention in her earlier statement having grabbed her assailant's testicles? 'Sometimes I get flashbacks of things that happened,' was the ingenuous reply.

The next day, Wednesday, 27 April, the dramatic events surrounding Robert Black's arrest held the court engrossed. It had been the watershed in the inquiry and it soon became apparent that it was a combination of luck and awareness that saved a six-year-old girl from becoming the fourth victim.

David Herkes, from the Border village of Stow recalled the sunny July day four years previously when he had been working in his garden. 'I saw a blue van pull up across the road near some children and the driver get out with a rag in his hand and open the passenger door. I also saw a child walking past the van but my view of the pavement was obstructed by the vehicle; I saw her legs and then they disappeared.. The driver was making a pushing motion into the van but the child never appeared in the seat. At that point I became suspicious.'

Herkes said that as the van drove away he had made a note of its index number and had then immediately informed the police and the parents of the little girl.

There is an old adage which says that when you want a policeman you can never find one. Fortunately on that July day in 1990 this did not apply; there were several police units not far away, and within minutes five or six panda cars and traffic patrol vehicles had converged on the village. While policeman were speaking to witnesses and relaying information back to their control room for circulation, the van reappeared. David Herkes: 'I shouted, "That's the van."'

During his trial so far Robert Black had only rarely displayed the slightest reaction to the proceedings; he seemed content to sit with his legs outstretched and his face expressionless. With the advent of the next witnesses this changed. For almost his entire adulthood he had lived with the Rayson family, eating and sleeping under the same roof, joining in their social life and playing with their children. Eventually he had been accepted as one of the family. Now, as Eddie and Kathy Rayson were followed by their sons into the witness box to testify for the prosecution, to Black it must have seemed the ultimate betrayal. His despondency was obvious as he shifted uncomfortably in his seat, glancing first at the ceiling and then down at his feet, before finally bending forward, his head resting between his hands.

The evidence of Raymond and John Rayson in particular was ill disposed towards their former lodger. Raymond recalled the day some seventeen years previously when he was sixteen and he and a young relative had entered Black's room during his absence. There they had looked inside a suitcase and found a number of pornographic photographs. 'What sort of people were depicted in the photographs?' asked John Milford. 'The majority of the photographs were of children,' Raymond told him. He said that he had also discovered a little girl's swimming costume in the suitcase. 'I was disgusted. I panicked and just had to get out of the room.'

John Rayson told the court that Black had frequently called at his Donisthorpe home near Burton-on-Trent. They had been out together drinking, and the court watched as a video film, which had been taken at the Raysons' twin daughters' fourth birthday party with Black clearly to be seen in the background, was shown. A friend of John Rayson's then remembered seeing Black at the Donisthorpe house during the weekend in mid-July 1983, at about the time Caroline Hogg's body was discovered a few miles away at Twycross.

The following morning it was again the turn of Toby Hedworth. The father of the little girl rescued at Stow, who like his daughter remained anonymous, was to be spared the ordeal of testifying. Instead his account of what had happened was read out by the barrister. After describing how he had stopped the blue Transit van and climbed into the back, the statement went on: 'The rear was almost empty. I reached out at what I first thought was a bundle of rags, but then realised that one of the items was a sleeping bag. I was calling for her and the sleeping bag moved.' There was dead silence in court as the father's emotions transmitted themselves through Mr Hedworth to those present. 'I then frantically tried to unwrap it and open it. I was speaking to her all the time. At first all I could see were her bare feet and legs . . . Her face was very red with the heat and there was a look of absolute terror on her face. Her mouth was bound and gagged, and her wrists were bound around her back . . .' Later, after being medically examined, his daughter had been able to point out the lay-by on the A7 where she said her kidnapper had taken her.

The prosecution was coming to an end with only the police evidence still to be heard. Detective Sergeant William Ormiston told how he had been accompanying Black in a police car back to Galashiels police station when his prisoner had said to him: 'What a day it's been. It should have happened on Friday the 13th. It was just a rush of blood. I have always been interested in young girls since I was a lad. I just saw her and got her into the van.'

Later during questioning at the police station about his afternoon's activities, Black had been asked whether he had assaulted the little girl. 'I didn't have much time,' he replied. 'It happened so quickly, I only touched her a little.' In answer to a further question he told detectives: 'I wanted to keep her and take her to somewhere like Blackpool for the weekend. I was going to drop her off later . . .' Mr Milford told the jury that Black later admitted having made all the remarks attributed to him except the one referring to Blackpool.

Before the next witness was called the jury were shown a number of items found in Black's van, and recovered from his London lodgings. These included a child's dress and swimming costume, a Polaroid camera and a roll of Elastoplast from the Transit van, together with porno-graphic books, films and videos, three scrapbooks of pornographic pic-tures and forty-eight copies of a magazine called *Unsolved*, from his room.

Detective Superintendent Peter Herward of Staffordshire Police went into the witness box to tell of his attempted interview with Black con-cerning the abduction and murder of Susan Maxwell. Black, however, had exercised his right to silence and had refused to answer questions. Herward went on to give some idea of the extent of the inquiry: 'It was a mammoth inquiry. Over the years we have recorded details of over 57,000 people who have come to our notice,' he said.

Ronald Thwaites asked him about a salesman dubbed Mr X who had become a suspect after being convicted in 1984 of sex offences against his two daughters. After agreeing that such had been the case, the Detective Superintendent went on to say that both he and the Crown Prosecution Service had come to the conclusion that there was insufficient evidence to prosecute.

The final day of the prosecution case conveniently preceded the start of the May Day bank holiday weekend. During the day the evidence of several detectives from different forces bore testimony to the scope of the investigation. Detective Chief Inspector Roger Orr, together with his Lothian and Borders colleague Detective Superintendent Andrew Watt, had interviewed Robert Black at St Leonard's police station in Edinburgh. Subsequently DCI Orr had led the painstaking and lengthy inquiries into Black's nationwide travels.

John Milford asked Detective Inspector Peter Robinson from West

Yorkshire about vehicles that had not been traced during the Sarah Harper inquiry. Robinson told him that only about thirty out of 1300 green Saabs – a car seen in Morley on the night Sarah had disappeared – had not been tracked down, but that it had proved impossible to trace a red Ford Escort which had also been seen due to there being about half a million such models in the country.

From Nottinghamshire Detective Superintendent Harry Shepherd explained that when reinvestigating the Teresa Thornhill incident following Black's arrest, out of fairness to the prisoner he had not put him on an identification parade as he understood that Miss Thornhill may have recently seen his photograph on television.

Finally Hector Clark (El Supremo), the Deputy Chief Constable of Lothian and Borders Police, formerly Assistant Chief Constable of Northumbria Police, told Mr Milford that Black was never among the 'tens of thousands' of people whom police had interviewed over almost eight years. He explained that it was only after Black had been arrested following the Stow kidnapping in 1990 that he had first come to police attention. Mr Clark went on to tell of the 189,000 people who had featured in the inquiry and the 22 tons of paperwork that had been generated. He could not recall any other cases in which children were abducted, killed and then transported considerable distances. The features were unique in his experience. Asked about the scale of the police inquiry he opined: 'I don't believe there has been a bigger crime investigation in the United Kingdom ever.'

As the court adjourned and those taking part together with observers of the trial dispersed into the cool evening air until the following Wednesday, there was an opportunity to assess the prosecution case. It was impressive, and being circumstantial arguably increased its credibility. The fact that there had been no recourse to identification or forensics ensured that all the evidence had been meticulously accumulated and prepared before being submitted to the Crown Prosecution Service.

After the jury had departed Mr Thwaites stood up and made application to have the charges against his client dismissed, submitting that the prosecution had failed to establish that he had a case to answer. Mr Justice Macpherson would have none of it, however, ruling that the prosecution case was such that it could only properly be decided by a jury. It was a forlorn if predictable defence tactic, the judge's rejection of which ensured that the following week Black's lawyers would have to present their case. They were faced with a formidable task, but having an advocate of Ronald Thwaites' calibre and experience as the leader of the defence meant that Robert Black was not without hope.

After a bank holiday weekend overshadowed by the death at the San Marino Grand Prix of three-times world formula one motor-racing champion Ayrton Senna and his fellow driver Roland Ratsenberger, the trial of Robert Black resumed on Wednesday, 4 May 1994, its fourteenth day.

Defence

Ronald Thwaites was to have to call heavily upon his oratorical skill in his defence of Black. There was a feeling of expectation in court as he stood up, adjusted his glasses and turned to face the jury. He reminded them that for eight years police had been investigating unsolved child abductions and murders before the arrest of Black in 1990 for the abduction of the child at Stow. 'How many reputations have been broken during that time?' he asked. 'No one knows, but you may think this series of cases reeks of failure, disappointment and frustration, brought to an end, they had hoped, by the capture of Black, who is brought before you as the murderer for all seasons.'

This was to be a recurring theme throughout the defence case: attacking the police, criticising the prosecution and trying to cast doubt on the motives and veracity of both. 'What relief bordering on euphoria the combined police forces must have felt when they arrested him in 1990 . . .' Here Ronald Thwaites was correct; there had certainly been overwhelming relief when Black was captured in July 1990 with his victim alive, but the feeling of elation had not emerged until it had become apparent that Black was the man police had for so long been seeking.

Mr Thwaites went on to claim that the police had got it wrong. 'This case has been developed before you using one incident of abduction in Stow, which Black admitted, as a substitute for evidence in all these other cases. There is no direct evidence against Black.' Again this was only partly true: there was no direct evidence, but the case against Robert Black had surely evolved from far more than the single incident at Stow.

Throughout his counsel's opening address Black had remained unmoved. Even when Mr Thwaites handed copies of his criminal record to the jury there was no reaction. Referring to his client's appearance at the High Court in Edinburgh for the Stow abduction, Mr Thwaites said:

'The judge saw fit to give him a life sentence; no one can be surprised by that and everyone must applaud it . . . Black's unhealthy lifelong interest in children is further confirmed by the haul of pornography found in his home. But although Black was a wicked and foul pervert, it did not follow that he was necessarily also a murderer. The question for you to decide is whether it may be proved he graduated from molester to murderer. There is nothing automatic about that.'

Towards the end of his opening speech Ronald Thwaites took a final swipe at the prosecution team and at the police. 'This case has not been presented in a straightforward manner . . . the prosecution has lost its way, wilfully blind to any other possibilities . . . this failure had dogged the footsteps of policemen over the years . . . There isn't the beginning of a case against him . . .' With a final flourish of his arm he told the jury: 'No one wants to be a witness for Mr Black; they do not want to come to give evidence for this wretched man. No one wants to be his friend. If they do not want to come we will serve them with summonses, and if necessary we will drag them in chains into this court,' a promise that brought a rare smile to the court.

Black was not to be called upon to give evidence on his own behalf. 'No man can be expected to remember the ordinary daily routine of his life going back many years . . .' said Mr Thwaites. Instead witnesses were to be called who presumably had that power of recall.

For the next five days, excluding the weekend, the defence witnesses testified. Much of what they said referred to believed sightings of Susan Maxwell on the afternoon of her disappearance, and to a red or dark-coloured saloon motor car seen in the vicinity of either Coldstream, the lay-by where Susan's body had been found, or near Sarah Harper's home at Morley. These were matters that had been thoroughly investigated and found wanting in some respect by the police.

An example was that of Thomas Ball, a psychiatric nurse, who told of seeing a maroon or dark-coloured Triumph saloon near the spot from where Susan Maxwell had been abducted. Ball had noticed that it appeared to contain at least two men, and that a child wearing a light T-shirt, and either shorts or a short skirt, was also present and seemed to be striking the vehicle with a tennis racket. Mr Thwaites claimed that this evidence in particular pointed away from Black. The next day other witnesses were to give evidence which in part corroborated that of Ball.

Joan Jones and her husband had been driving along the A518 on the evening of Susan Maxwell's disappearance when she had noticed a dark-coloured car with a man next to it in the Loxley lay-by. 'As soon as the man saw us he quickly put his head into the car . . . I just thought he was rather suspicious. I wondered if he was dumping rubbish.'

The intervening weekend saw the death of another sportsman. Jockey Steve Wood died following a fall during a race at Lingfield Park. There was news also of the Conservative Party's attempts to reconcile them-selves to the recent local council election setback. Meanwhile the Robert Black jury were maybe thinking that the defence evidence they had so far heard made a conviction of the accused by no means a foregone conclu-sion.

On Monday Mr Thwaites called a young woman to give evidence who had been only thirteen years old at the time of which she spoke. Michelle Robertson had been playing with other children in the park near Caroline Hogg's home between 3 p.m. and 4 p.m. on Friday, 8 July 1983. She told Mr Thwaites, 'There was a man in the park on his own who was a bit strange-looking. He was about mid-forties to fifty and had on a dark mac, dark trousers and a white shirt. He looked a bit scruffy in appearance . . . There were lots of children playing on the roundabout. I noticed a girl with blonde hair in bunches. She had a dress on and white socks and sandals . . . The man was looking over in her direction a lot.'

According to the witness when the group of children left the park the man had followed them. She added that she had also seen an old navy blue Ford Escort-type car in Portobello that had attracted her notice.

Making allowance for the length of time that had elapsed, Michelle Robertson's recollection of the man and the girl she had seen in the park could easily have applied to Robert Black and Caroline Hogg. There did appear to be a discrepancy between the times she had given and the time mentioned by Annette Hogg, and her reference to the Ford motor car seemed a likely red herring.

Similarly the evidence of Kevin Catherall and Ian Collins, both of whom said that they had seen red Ford cars in Morley on the night of Sarah Harper's disappearance; neither man's story did much to further the likelihood that the car's occupants had been in any way involved in the girl's abduction.

The last two defence witnesses to testify on Tuesday had also noticed a red or maroon saloon car in Morley that evening. Again neither Alan Day nor Peter Armstrong's testimony put forward a credible alternative suspect. Day had seen a Datsun-style car containing a man and a woman stop and apparently try to engage a small boy in conversation, while

Armstrong had noticed a maroon saloon car, and two children who he thought may have been girls walking nearby. It seemed to observers that both witnesses had been called solely in an attempt to divert suspicion away from Robert Black.

As Ronald Thwaites sat down Black had cause to be satisfied, knowing that his team of lawyers had done their best on his behalf. Several witnesses had spoken of people and situations that could be said to be suspicious. The question remained: would the defence case be strong enough to rebut the prosecution's claims, and raise that doubt in the jury's minds necessary to secure Black's acquittal? That would not have to be considered by the men and women sitting a few feet away until after counsel's closing speeches and Mr Justice Macpherson's summing-up. In the meantime the trial was adjourned until Thursday, allowing all those participating an unexpected respite from their responsibilities.

Two days later when the court reassembled, everyone present knew that the trial was entering its closing phase. The day was to be taken up with John Milford's closing speech in which he was to bring together the various aspects of the prosecution case. This, it was hoped, would remove doubt or ambiguity from the jury's mind. Despite the mass of circumstantial evidence linking Robert Black with the crimes, much of which was supported by the corroborative testimony of witnesses, there remained what could turn out to be critical shortcomings in the case.

It had failed to produce a direct link between Black and the abduction and murders of Susan Maxwell, Caroline Hogg or Sarah Harper. The only direct evidence relevant to the commission by him of an offence against a child was the attack on Teresa Thornhill, and the items found in the back of his van at Stow. That was an offence which Mr Thwaites had been obliged to acknowledge had resulted in life imprisonment for Black. Furthermore, despite meticulous tests and examinations carried out by a team of scientists on many items connected to Black or his victims, nothing forensically had been found to link him with the crimes. The prosecution team were nonetheless confident that the mass of circumstantial evidence, accumulated since 1990, would enable them to secure the conviction of the man sitting in the dock.

John Milford opened his final address to the jury by referring to Black's arrest in 1990 when he had been caught almost red-handed abducting a girl in Stow. 'What he was about to do, as you can reasonably infer from the evidence, doesn't just prove he was a bad man, a paedophile, a child molester, it actually proves he committed these other offences. His arrest had been the beginning of a lifetime of incarceration and ended a series of offences which are unlikely ever to be forgotten and which represent man at his most vile.'

Drawing the jury's attention to the 'collective circumstantial evidence', Mr Milford told them that 'We submit this evidence of a character sufficiently special as to reasonably identify him as committing the other crimes . . . they are all so strikingly similar that they bear Black's hallmarks.'

The defence argument that Black's proximity when the crimes were committed was mere coincidence would, if correct, 'be the coincidence to end all coincidences', said the prosecutor. He went on: 'The similarities outnumber the dissimilarities. One element welds them together as unsolved crimes, that is the long distance the bodies were taken . . . his presence at all these scenes is not a coincidence . . . to suggest it is, is an affront to common sense, the most important sense you will use in this case.'

Turning to Black's involvement in the crimes, Mr Milford said that after being arrested at the border he had told a policeman that it was '"a rush of blood". It was no "rush of blood",' said John Milford scathingly. 'He had come prepared, having with him in his van sticking plaster to use as a gag, cord to bind his victim, a cushion cover and those revolting probes.'

Continuing on the same theme John Milford declared: 'What he did demonstrates a quite appalling capacity for cruelty.' As to what would have been the little girl's fate at Stow if she had not been rescued, the prosecutor was in no doubt. 'There is no need to speculate as to what he would have done with her, what her ultimate fate would have been in the hands of one so callous and cruel. When she had served her purpose, would someone have found her alive?' he asked. '. . . Would a man of Black's background have left her as living evidence of his misdeed, to describe him and lead to his arrest and conviction? No,' said the Crown advocate emphatically. 'What we would have found is another decomposing little body with no socks and no shoes.'

Prosecuting counsel admitted that, despite their unremitting efforts, the time gaps had frustrated the forensic scientists in their bid to find a link between Black and the murder victims. 'What was the chance of them ever doing so?' he asked.

When John Milford sat down at the end of his speech, it was agreed that his had been a carefully balanced exposition, covering all aspects of the case against Black before leaving it to the jury to consider and evalu-

ate his submissions. Before then they would listen to the defence arguments advanced by Ronald Thwaites.

The national press on the morning of Friday, 13 May 1994, was devoted
almost exclusively to the death of the Labour Party leader John Smith
who had died in St Bartholomew's Hospital the previous evening soon
after having suffered a heart attack at his nearby Barbican flat. At the
Moot Hall in Newcastle, with the trial entering upon its final stage, much
of the court-room chatter prior to the opening of the proceedings was
about the man who had himself been a successful advocate at the Scottish
Bar before entering Parliament.

In was day twenty of the trial, the day that Ronald Thwaites was to set
about the formidable task of combating the prosecution case. The pre-
trial decision by Mr Justice Macpherson to allow evidence surrounding
the circumstances of the Stow abduction to be admitted, meant that Mr
Thwaites had to concede early on that his client was 'a wicked and foul
pervert', sexually obsessed with young girls, and quite capable of attacking and sexually assaulting them.

'Where is the jury that will acquit a pervert of multiple murder?' he
asked. '. . . this is an unpopular course for this disgusting man . . . He is
on the scrap heap. He has only served four years of a life sentence . . . the
teeth of the children are hanging around his neck. There will be no cam-
paign for his release if you convict him . . . Black's acquittal will not be
greeted with applause. It is a real test of the jury to convict on flimsy or
no evidence.'

The uncompromising start to his speech by defending counsel must
have caused the jury to speculate as to where his allegiance lay. The
problem facing Ronald Thwaites was with the jury; being aware of
Black's 1990 conviction, they nevertheless had to be convinced that his
base instincts did not extend beyond sexually assaulting his victims, and
that he would draw a line at killing them.

Mr Thwaites continued: 'Before you convict him someone must show
that behind his impassive stare lurks a killer's profile . . . that his unique
signature is all over these murders . . . he is the pervert against whom there
is only prejudice, but no hard evidence.' Black's advocate cautioned the
jury against being influenced by public opinion, or by 'polluted, if not
completely poisonous' remarks in the press. He insisted that 'a vote for
Black would be a vote for the jury system'.

It was an impassioned appeal, made with all the fervour and conviction of which Ronald Thwaites was capable. The contrast with his

opponent was marked: John Milford, painstaking, restrained, presenting the facts; Thwaites, despite arguing from a defensive viewpoint, confident and assertive, pressing upon the jury the necessity to differentiate between a sexual pervert and an alleged child murderer.

He was scathing in his dismissal of Hugh Crystal's testimony: 'He was like a robot giving evidence. He was hopeless, wasn't he?' Predictably also he attacked the police investigation: 'If you convict him of this horrible catalogue of crimes it will certainly make a lot of people feel a lot more comfortable . . .' he said. Acquittal would require the police to reopen the case 'and perhaps somewhere in the 22 tons of evidence collected there may lurk the real killers. Black is needed as a painless solution to an irksome problem . . . created by the police and their over-active dirty tricks department.'

A senior police officer to whom I spoke told me that, despite their professionalism, detectives felt anger and resentment at what they considered to be unfair and unwarranted attacks and criticism. 'There was no way we could respond. We just had to accept the remarks.'

The defence advocate made a final thrust: 'The police have become exhausted in not finding anyone,' he declared. 'The public are clamouring for a result . . . what good are you if you can't catch a child killer? . . . The police were under continuing unbearable pressure, then they find Mr Black. Is he their salvation, or a convenient expendable scapegoat?'

When finally he sat down, Ronald Thwaites had reason to feel satisfied that he had effectively put forward a credible argument on behalf of his client. The lack of direct or forensic evidence, public and media prejudice, the weaknesses of the Crown case, together with what he considered to be the shortcomings in the police investigation: all these factors he had exploited. In addition he had maintained that the defence witnesses pointed to someone else being the killer.

It remained now for Mr Justice Macpherson to sum up. To clarify the law and ensure that the jury were in possession of the facts and understood the various points that had been made for and against the accused. The judge announced that his summing-up would commence after the weekend.

The morning of Monday, 16 May 1994, saw No. 1 Court at the Moot Hall packed with those anxious to hear Mr Justice Macpherson start his summing-up of a trial that had been followed avidly by millions of people since it had opened almost five weeks earlier. During that time dozens of witnesses had been heard, a mass of evidence had been submitted for the jury to consider, and the lawyers had argued their respective cases with all the advocatory skill at their command. It was now the turn of the man who had presided over the proceedings.

In his book *Fear the Stranger*, Hector Clark described Mr Justice Macpherson as a 'warm and friendly individual who presided in a business-like and impressive manner'. Careful always to ensure the jury's comfort, he dignified with firmness his judicial role. This he had demonstrated with his earlier rulings when he had refused to allow either a transcript of Black's Edinburgh interview with Andrew Watt and Roger Orr, or his replies when the summonses had been served on him in Peterhead Prison, to be admitted in evidence.

It was the first occasion on which the parents of the victims were together in court. With the exception of Jackie Harper they had previously stayed away, preferring not to hear the harrowing details surrounding their own personal tragedy. Now, with the evidence all heard, they were at the Moot Hall for the trial's concluding phase. Sitting alongside each other in the front row of the public gallery, they had a clear view of the court, and of Robert Black sitting in the dock.

Mr Justice Macpherson opened his address by referring to the thousands of statements taken, vehicles investigated and documents accumulated during the police inquiry. 'My own reaction was relief to know that such thoroughness was shown in an inquiry of this kind, and not criticism,' he said.

Referring to evidence that showed Black had had a lifetime interest in young girls and paedophile pornography, the judge went on to warn the jury against convicting him of murder 'because of his habits and proven obsession with young girls'. He warned further against assuming that because of the circumstances and life sentence which had resulted from the Stow incident, Black was necessarily guilty of the murders of Susan Maxwell, Caroline Hogg and Sarah Harper.

'You must not give a dog a bad name and hang him for that reason alone, although you may apply the facts of the Stow case to the facts of these other investigations.' The Crown had said that the incident 'provides a link which forms the eventual chain in this case and the specimen signature which illuminates the whole line of awful crimes we have investigated in this court room'. The jury would have to consider whether the three murders with which he was charged bore Black's 'signature or hallmark'.

Mr Justice Macpherson trenchantly referred to some of the defence observations: 'I have not observed dirty tricks by the Crown, nor bad faith over documents . . . The whole basis of the defence was essentially to discredit the police; to confuse the jury with red herrings, and by criticism of the conduct of the case'.

The victims' families listened attentively as the judge continued: 'The palpable availability of Black is a remarkable feature of this case, including the distribution of the bodies in the Midlands . . . it is for you (the jury) to decide whether or not the long arm of coincidence can be stretched this long.' Referring to the murder of Sarah Harper he said: 'It is an affront to common sense that the similarities with this case when compared with the others could be coincidence at all.'

There was scarcely any movement in court as Mr Justice Macpherson was speaking; lawyers, policemen and reporters listened attentively to his every word. The jury, acutely conscious of their responsibility, never let their attention waver for a moment while he was speaking.

Reaffirming Black's entitlement to remain silent, Mr Justice Macpherson made it clear 'that it does not mean in any way that he is guilty because of his silence. It means you simply do not have the facts from him.' Referring to the conflicting identification evidence, the judge remarked cannily: 'Identification means who he was rather than what he looked like.'

The trial judge accepted that much of the evidence relating to Black's fuel purchases, and his poster deliveries, vital though it was in pin-pointing his journeyings, did not need to be unduly dwelt upon: '. . . it seems to me that the exacting and detailed evidence proves the transactions, and brackets the time . . . I am convinced that examination of petrol receipts and posters would be tedious and unnecessary . . . As a matter of common sense, inference and proper deduction, he was at Portobello and Stafford, and available to go to Twycross.'

Finally Mr Justice Macpherson reminded the jury that feelings during the trial had often run high. 'We must restrain ourselves from strong emotion in a case of this kind although that may be difficult to do . . . Firmness, fairness and justice must be the hallmarks of your decision . . . Look at the whole picture and all the evidence . . . do not be swayed by small singular disagreements. Guilt on one charge must not allow you to assume guilt on the others . . . There is no substitute for a cool hard realistic look at all of the evidence you have heard. Are you sure that the interlocking and similarities of all these cases drives you to the conclusion that this man Robert Black is guilty in these four cases, or set of cases before you?'

Mr Justice Macpherson did not finish summing up until mid-afternoon on Monday, so he decided then to send the jury home until the following morning. This would enable them to commence their deliberations after a night's rest. Soon after they had reassembled the next day, the jury retired to their room to commence their decision-making. After the judge had also risen and left the court room, a buzz of conversation ensued.

A unique atmosphere pervades a court of law at this stage. For days, sometimes weeks, lawyers have questioned and cross-examined witnesses, advanced theories and argued their case. The witnesses in their turn have suffered from varying degrees of nervousness, but have as a rule tried to answer truthfully questions relating to events that have sometimes occurred months, even years before. Now, with the summing-up over and the jury having left the court, laywers, policemen, witnesses and others connected with, or having a close interest in, the case assume an attitude which is part relaxed, part tense and expectant.

The Maxwell, Hogg and Harper families together in the public gallery chatted nervously, while lawyers, detectives and court officials spoke among themselves. As the hours passed tension increased among the policemen, journalists and others mingling in the Moot Hall foyer; while they discussed the possible outcome of the trial, reporters on mobile telephones updated their newspapers on the latest situation.

After six hours, when word came that the jury were deadlocked and were to be accommodated overnight in a local hotel, feelings varied from anxiety over the significance of this development, to a philosophical acceptance of the situation. Some felt that the delay augered well for Black, while others saw it as reflecting the difficulties confronting the members of the jury as they tried to resolve the complexities of the case, and their determination to come to the correct decision.

Before they departed for their hotel, Mr Justice Macpherson cautioned the six men and six women jury members against reading newspapers, watching television or making telephone calls. They faced a night of isolation under the watchful eyes of two court bailiffs. The judge further warned media representatives against trying to contact or photograph the jurors on pain of appearing before him for contempt of court.

On Wednesday morning the court was again full in anticipation of there being a result. Before they continued with their deliberations, Mr Justice Macpherson urged the jury to reach a unanimous decision, but added that if that proved to be impossible, he would accept a 10–2 majority verdict.

For a second day the hours dragged by. Conversation was muted. The faces of the victims' relatives betrayed the strain they were under; lawyers occasionally exchanged words, while detectives, although appearing outwardly calm, felt increasingly tense as the day wore on. Superintendent Peter Herward from Staffordshire was feeling distraught by mid-afternoon, 'fearing the worst'. His sympathy lay with the jury: 'When you have a case of such complexity, how can twelve men and women good and true that are called from various backgrounds and with varying knowledge – how can we expect them to resolve such issues when it has taken us years to put it together and to get an understanding?'

At last in the afternoon word came that the jury were about to return. Lawyers, detectives and others hastened back to their seats only to experience another anti-climax as the jury foreman announced that they were still unable to reach a verdict. It's the amount of evidence there is to examine, he explained apologetically to the judge. Mr Justice Macpherson was understanding. Assuring the jury that they need not feel under any pressure, he told the foreman, 'I absolutely understand the position and don't worry. There is a great deal of evidence you must go through with all the care you wish.'

Thus encouraged, the jury went back to their hotel for another night. Meanwhile few there were who spared a thought for Robert Black as he was driven through the side gate of the Moot Hall, his fate still unknown. A cluster of press photographers snatched pictures as they ran alongside the closed police van as it started on its journey back to Durham Prison.

When the court reconvened at 10 a.m. on Thursday, 19 May 1994, there was an underlying feeling that the day would see the culmination of the proceedings. After the usual preliminaries the jury retired for the third time. However, today they were only absent for just over an hour before a bailiff re-entered the court room and, going across to Mr Bean, whispered to him that the jury were about to return. The room became alive with police, lawyers and reporters hurrying back to their places. After the jury had filed back into court, Mr Justice Macpherson entered and resumed his seat. After asking everyone to remain silent while the verdicts were announced, Mr Bean ordered Black to stand up and then turned to the foreman of the jury. Yes, they had agreed their verdict on all ten charges. There was total silence in the court room as, in reply to each charge, the foreman spoke the single word, 'Guilty.' Half-way through the announcements Elizabeth Maxwell broke down sobbing; her husband Fordyce somehow managed to contain his emotion.

As the verdict was announced respecting Caroline Hogg, her mother, sitting in the front row of the public gallery, allowed a slight smile of satisfaction to creep across her face. Jackie Harper sat weeping, her head in her hands, as Black was found guilty of the abduction and murder of her daughter. Two women members of the jury also wept silently. Robert Black stared straight ahead, as inscrutable as ever.

After the foreman of the jury had sat down at the end of his announcement, Mr Justice Macpherson turned to the man facing him in the dock. The dramatic impact of his next words was not lessened even though there was already a noticeable easing of the tension in court.

'Robert Black, you have said nothing in court. Neither you nor the public will expect me to say more than a few words in sentence. You are an extremely dangerous man . . . I sentence you on each of these counts to life imprisonment. In respect of each of these ten counts I expect you will be detained for the whole of your life, but on the murder counts I propose to make a public recommendation that the minimum time for which you be detained is thirty-five years on each of the murder convictions. Take him down.'

It was over; Black had remained unmoved during his sentencing. Only as he was about to leave the dock did he speak. Turning to the detectives sitting behind him he said mockingly, 'Well done, boys.' It was a frivolous remark uttered in a spirit of bravado, but it could be said to reflect the sentiments not only of the Maxwells, Hoggs and Harpers, but of the millions of other parents of little girls. Now they could rest secure in the knowledge that such an evil predator was no longer free to prey on their children.

CHAPTER 15

THE AFTERMATH

While Robert Black was calmly drinking a cup of tea in his cell in the court basement while awaiting conveyance to a dispersal prison, police officers in the case prepared to face the media representatives who were assembled outside.

The trial had attracted worldwide attention throughout, but now on the final day the newsmen and women excelled themselves. Every available vantage point within a hundred yards of the Moot Hall had been taken up by reporters, photographers and television crews. The court foyer was a scene of confusion as lawyers, policemen, court officials and members of the public, reminiscent of the opening day of the trial, got in the way of reporters anxious to interview the main participants as they emerged.

Outside, a dozen television vans were already strategically placed with satellite aerials and link lines to studios protruding from the vehicles, while a score of press photographers vied with each other at the Moot Hall gates to obtain the best vantage points. The most resourceful cameramen, equipped with high-powered lenses, positioned themselves on the castle ramparts overlooking the court. From there they had an unrestricted view of the activity below. It was the biggest media invasion since the first day of the trial.

As Hector Clark, Roger Orr, Andrew Brown and a score of other policemen emerged from the court room, the reporters and photographers converged on them. Easing their way through the crowd, the officers saved their comments until they were outside the building.

'The tragedy is these three beautiful children who should never have died,' Clark told reporters. 'Black is the most evil of characters and I hope there is not now or ever another one like him . . .'

Andrew Brown, the Lothian and Borders Assistant Chief Constable, voiced the compassionate feelings of them all when he pointed out that 'Over the years, the families of the girls have had constant reminders of their loss and the trauma must have been enormous . . . Our thoughts are with them today, as they have always been . . .'

Both Clark and Brown were generous in their praise of those who had worked alongside them on the inquiry. Andrew Brown referred to Hector Clark's 'dedication and professionalism', while in turn Clark gave credit to 'the excellent detectives from six forces who had worked together over many years . . . the result today is a total justification and vindication of their effort.'

Dennis Cleugh was another policeman who had been a participant in the Black inquiry since 1982, when as a detective sergeant he had been the Northumbrian Police force liaison officer. Later he had become involved both with the Caroline Hogg investigation, and with the Child Murder Bureau at Bradford.

Following promotion to Detective Inspector and then to Detective Chief Inspector, Cleugh continued his association with the inquiry which by the late 1980s embraced the Morley abduction and subsequent murder of Sarah Jane Harper. With promotion had come increased responsibility; while continuing in his role as liaison officer, Cleugh became increasingly involved not only in the investigative aspects of inquiries, interviewing suspects and following up leads while still with the Northumbrian Police crime squad, but also with the strategic planning of the overall operation. In 1988 he attended a conference at Peebles to discuss the future of the Child Murder Bureau, and thenceforth he was regularly present at senior officer conferences and planning meetings. With Detective Chief Inspector Roger Orr prior to the trial, Cleugh helped in setting up the Pilgrim Street incident room at Newcastle upon Tyne, and he later attended the trial.

Dennis Cleugh was one of many policemen who devoted over a third of their service to the Robert Black case. They had other work responsibilities and commitments but these were largely overshadowed by the murder inquiry. In a reference to the spirit of co-operation that existed between the forces he said: 'I initially worked long and unsocial hours with a number of officers, some now retired, some now dead . . . We dealt with many suspects, and experienced many disappointments over the years, but we were all involved in some way and later represented our forces at Black's trial.'

Detective Constable Lindsey McBride of Lothian and Borders was on holiday in Florida when he learnt of the outcome of the trial: 'Although I had been involved in the investigation for several years I had never set eyes on Black since his capture in 1990. I was buying groceries at a local store in Florida when I caught sight of a copy of the previous day's *Daily Telegraph*. There was a picture of Robert Black in handcuffs on the front page, and next to it a big headline announcing that he had been given ten life sentences. It gave me a feeling right down my spine; it was a unique experience.'

The feelings of relief and euphoria at the result of the trial were not confined to the policemen. Inside the court building a room had been set aside for relatives of the victims, to enable them to digest the results and compose themselves before venturing forth to confront the reporters and photographers waiting outside. For all of them it had been a long wait. They had shared the police frustration and disappointment over the years as their early optimism faded, but like the detectives they had never given up hope that one day the person responsible for the deaths of their children would have to answer for his crimes.

All three families had moved home since their personal tragedy had struck them. The Maxwells had given up farming in 1988 and moved from Cramond Hill farm with their other children, Jacqueline and Tom, to a comfortable detached house in Berwick-upon-Tweed. Both Elizabeth and Fordyce Maxwell have there resumed their former occupation as journalists. John and Annette Hogg moved from Beach Lane, Portobello, to a three-bedroomed detached house in another part of the town. Neither of them ever spoke publicly of their grief after their brief television and newspaper appeals soon after their daughter had gone missing, preferring to keep their feelings to themselves. They struck up a strong rapport with Hector Clark who kept in regular contact and helped to sustain them. Jackie Harper, supported by her mother Marlene Hopton, survived a broken marriage and later moved to Heckmondwike, a few miles from Morley. There she lives with Tony Salisbury and her three other children.

Now, at the conclusion of the trial, they all nerved themselves to face the media representatives. Emerging into the courtyard in front of the Moot Hall, each was to make only a brief comment. Elizabeth Maxwell, who was later to make a fuller statement, confined herself to saying that 'Every parent in this country can rest more easily knowing that Robert Black is in gaol for the rest of his life.'

A tearful Jackie Harper and Annette Hogg were similarly brief and incisive. Jackie, who said that the verdict was 'brilliant', added that the only time Black should leave prison was in a wooden box. 'He should be put in a 6 ft by 6 ft cell with a straw mattress, with no newspapers, television or comforts.' Her mother went on, 'To see him hanged would be too quick; I want him to suffer torment the way those three children have.'

Annette Hogg's verdict was terse: 'I'm very relieved,' was all she said before she was hurried away with the other families to waiting cars.

With the police officers, witnesses and relatives departing, the reporters and photographers also hastened away to write up their news reports and file their copy for the evening or following morning's editions of their papers. Television crews meanwhile dismantled their equipment and stowed it away in their vehicles before they too left the court precincts for the last time.

Leaving the court almost unnoticed, accompanied by her partner Paul and her parents Brian and Ruby, Teresa Thornhill, who so narrowly escaped becoming Robert Black's fourth fatal victim, paused long enough to tell reporters of her relief: 'Thank God it's over and he'll never walk the streets again. It's been a terrible wait, but now I feel it's been worthwhile. Already some of the pain seems to be lifting, but even thirty-five years isn't long enough.'

Elsewhere, as news of the verdict spread, similar sentiments were expressed. Those of two of his former drinking companions in Stoke Newington were typical. 'They should never let him out; what are those kids' parents going to think if he's out walking the streets again in ten or fifteen years?' was the question posed by Stanley Ottoway. Trevor Rigby shared his friend's views: 'Some men are so bad that they just aren't fit to be let out.' In a note of cynicism he added, 'I expect in years to come memory of what he's done will start to fade, but I think he should be kept in like those two who did the Moors murders.'

Later on that final afternoon Elizabeth Maxwell, with her husband Fordyce sitting alongside her, faced reporters once more. She expressed her relief at the verdict, 'a just and right decision', adding, '. . . we have had a long wait for it.' She went on to pay tribute to Mr Justice Macpherson for his careful and considered advice to the jury which, she said, 'was tinged with good old-fashioned common sense'. Allied to this comment were thanks to the jury for coming 'to the right and just decision' after their long deliberations.

Elizabeth Maxwell reserved her greatest praise for the police for the manner in which they had conducted the long inquiry which, she said, 'at times must have been mind-numbing for them . . . They must feel almost more relief than we do after twelve years of investigation. There might be some criticism of them, questions asked why Robert Black was not caught sooner, but that would not have saved Susan or Caroline or Sarah.' She continued, 'This is not *Inspector Morse*, this is real life, and it has been painstaking detective work, including a team who have studied millions of petrol receipts, to pin down the crucial evidence.'

Her words must have delighted all officers who had been on the inquiry, but none more so than Hector Clark who had borne the brunt of the criticism from both inside and outside the police. Nevertheless, now that the trial was over, and Robert Black was safely back in prison, there to remain for the foreseeable future, several issues had arisen which are worthy of closer examination.

First, mention should be made of Black's application for leave to appeal against his conviction. On Monday, 20 February 1995, he appeared at the Court of Appeal before the Lord Chief Justice, Lord Taylor of Gosforth, sitting with Mr Justice Ognall and Mrs Justice Steel. Ronald Thwaites was appearing for the appellant. Also present were several senior detectives, ostensibly maintaining a watching brief, but inwardly wondering if their years of effort were to be later negated by the court's decision.

The submissions made by Ronald Thwaites were, to a certain degree, predictable, based as they largely were on the defence entered at the trial. He argued that Black had been denied a fair trial because of a faulty legal ruling and an 'unbalanced' summing-up by the trial judge. The defence team, he said, fundamentally disagreed with Mr Justice Macpherson's ruling that details of Robert Black's arrest in July 1990 for abducting and sexually assaulting a six-year-old girl at Stow in Scotland were admissible as 'similar fact' evidence, and that there was therefore a 'common signature' indicating the possibility of a single offender.

The lawyer pointed out that there were more differences than significant points in common. He argued that there was a wide variation in the victims' ages, five and fifteen (the age of Teresa Thornhill), that the manner and location of the abductions were different, and that the methods of killing and disposal of the bodies did not bear the hallmark of one perpetrator. The suggestion that Mr Justice Macpherson's summing-up had been unbalanced was difficult to sustain in the opinion of most observers. It had generally been considered at the time, and later upon reflection, a model of judicial excellence.

The appeal hearing had been scheduled to last for three days, but at the end of the first day Lord Taylor announced that they were refusing leave to appeal against the conviction. Ronald Thwaites had done his best, but the court's decision may not have altogether surprised him. As for Black, he had remained inscrutable throughout the hearing and showed no emotion as he left the dock to return to prison and resume his sentence.

Serial murder or multiple homicide is by definition a progression from a single killing. In multiple child murders an individual feels impelled after having claimed his first victim to seek out others. What is the motivating force that precipitates such action? This is a problem for which psychiatrists and other experts are continually seeking an answer.

In the case of adult homicides the motive is often readily apparent; sexual desire, greed, jealousy and simple hatred are among the more familiar reasons put forward for taking another person's life. The influence of drink or drugs is another common reason advanced as the driving force by defence lawyers, often with no compelling rationale behind the crime other than some imagined slight in the perpetrator's mind enhanced by alcohol, or an irresistible desire to replenish a drug supply, or obtain the wherewithal so to do.

With a child killer the motive is frequently obscured under an umbrella of theories relating to an individual's early background and experiences, and the influence these may have had in provoking acts of violence towards children in later life.

Few would disagree that sexual abuse and other deviant behaviour experienced as a child, and carried through to adolescence, can have a significant and deleterious bearing on later behaviour; but is this the only answer? Quite obviously not. Countless adults from every walk of life and stratum of society have at some time early in life been physically abused, or subjected to such indignities as indecent exposure, pornography or peer group pressure to indulge in experimental sexual activity. Such experiences, sometimes distasteful, sometimes not, have eventually faded in their memory, and if not completely forgotten have been looked back upon philosophically.

How did Robert Black fit into this formula? Long before there is evidence of any sexual abuse towards him he was sexually aware. When he started at Kinlochleven primary school while being fostered by Betty Tulip, apart from being aggressive towards other children, he was in the habit of lying on the ground to enable him to peer under little girls' skirts, while it was at about this time that he began to take an unhealthy view of his own body.

In Black's case, therefore, it would seem that his sexual curiosity and awareness were part of his genetic make-up. His instinctual sexual urgings appear to have manifested themselves during his early emotional development, but were not recognised or, if they were, no attempt was made to control or eradicate them. His sexual precocity, encouraged no doubt by the abuse to which he had been subjected while at the Red House Care Home, became firmly established, and was allowed to develop unhindered until his first court appearance in 1963.

By then Black's penchant for young females was irresistible. Although a psychiatrist's report was obtained by the court at the time, its assessment suggesting that the offence for which he was appearing was an isolated incident, and by inference one unlikely to be repeated, proved to be wildly over-optimistic. It was an opportunity missed; if Robert Black's wayward behaviour and deviant tendencies had been correctly assessed in 1963, it is possible that intensive therapy in a controlled environment could have diverted him from the lifestyle and the irrevocable course of action upon which he was to embark.

Instead Black's behaviour was to degenerate; the spell in Borstal seemed to have little effect. In London, fed on a diet of hard pornography, his waywardness continued. Eventually his desires could no longer be satisfied by simply indecently assaulting his victims. Only by abducting, ravishing and then killing them could he sate his dreadful appetite for little girls.

This brings into question Ray Wyre's intervention. On the days following Robert Black's conviction, tabloid newspaper headlines were lurid and sensational – 'Monster' was a popular word to describe him – and posed the question: 'How many other victims could be attributed to him?' Most papers also devoted several columns to Wyre's prison interviews with Black. However, space permitted the reporting of only a fraction of their dialogue. For over two years the interviews had been carried out, probing in considerable depth into Black's psyche. The newspaper extracts concentrated, as was to be expected, on only the most shocking and self-incriminatory aspect of the interviews. Similarly, the Channel 4 broadcast the day after Black's conviction was targeted at a mass audience and was necessarily restricted in its coverage.

A thorough account of the interviews, together with a résumé of

Robert Black's early life and upbringing, appeared in Ray Wyre's book *The Murder of Childhood* (Penguin, 1995). In it the author describes the founding and development of the Gracewell Clinic in Birmingham, his first meetings with Black and the subsequent development of their relationship.

It was learning that Ray Wyre's interviews with Black had taken place without his knowledge, and were only published and broadcast immediately following the end of the trial, that so aggrieved Hector Clark and his colleagues. Clark's displeasure is understandable; he and his fellow detectives had dealt with the consequences of Black's actions; had seen the lifeless bodies of his victims; had visited their distraught parents trying to find words of comfort. They had spent many years in tracking down a man, with the constant fear that he might strike again at any time.

Ray Wyre should have realised that the detectives investigating the crimes of Robert Black would have been extremely interested to learn at the time of some of his client's revelations. Wyre may in fact have been aware of this, but have decided for some reason that until it suited him details of the interviews would remain confidential. I have pointed out earlier that in my view neither the contents of Wyre's book, nor the newspaper or television extracts from it, disclosed anything that would have directly helped the police to secure Robert Black's conviction.

This poses another question: had Ray Wyre or any other psychiatrist had access to Black during his formative years, was it likely that their intervention would have altered the course of subsequent events?

This is impossible to answer. Wyre is acknowledged as an extremely able and experienced sexual therapist with a growing international reputation. He founded the Gracewell Clinic in 1988, an establishment that provided a therapeutic residential environment where child sex offenders and abusers, after confronting their attitude and offending pattern, would undergo intensive therapy and treatment. Additionally the clinic provided assessment reports of both convicted and unconvicted offenders.

During the five years of its existence the Gracewell Clinic treated hundreds of child sex offenders who might otherwise have been in the community, free to indulge unhindered in their paedophilia. During that time it is difficult to assess the clinic's success rate in terms of reoffending, but when it was closed in December 1993, as the result of irrational and ill-informed local prejudice, it undoubtedly signalled a victory to the 'lock 'em up and throw away the key' brigade, thereby abandoning any hope there may have been of reducing the offending pattern of known sex offenders.

It is arguable whether therapy at an early age would have altered Black's emotional development. Almost from infancy Robert Black had an unhealthy interest in sex, and was soon displaying a mature sexual awareness. Was therapy appropriate to one of tender years available? If so, it would need to have been carried out sympathetically by a therapist not only versed in sexual deviancy, but with the experience and ability to communicate effectively with the young.

Conversely it may be asked whether it was likely that intervention at any age would have been effective, or was Black innately evil? Flawed from birth, to grow up as Mr Justice Macpherson said when sentencing him, into 'an extremely dangerous man'. I leave the reader to judge.

Hector Clark admitted, 'I have always been prepared to accept criticism of my actions providing it is fair and constructive. What has irritated and hurt me has been ill-informed comment by the press and the media, and criticism by one or two colleagues who after working alongside me for so long, spoke out publicly without first discussing the issues with me.'

El Supremo's impatience with those who he thought had unfairly criticised him and other detectives after the trial was understandable. For years he and his team had dedicated themselves with infinite patience and single-minded determination to bringing about the arrest of an intelligent and elusive child killer.

Police officers involved in the investigation have never denied that it was sheer good fortune, allied to the observation and astuteness of a member of the public, that precipitated Robert Black's eventual apprehension. However, after the trial the circumstances of Black's capture, details of his life and background, together with descriptions of his crimes and the reaction of his victims' families to his conviction, dominated the headlines and reports in most newspapers, and over-shadowed accounts of the unparalleled police investigation.

This notwithstanding, a considerable number of column inches were devoted to criticism of the police investigation. Most dwelt on the time it had taken to bring Robert Black to justice, but there were references also to alleged mistakes and omissions that had occurred during the inquiry – all of it, of course, written in hindsight.

Examination of some of the supposed investigative shortcomings reveals that, rather than being errors or omissions, they refer to false or

aborted leads. Many times when following up or acting upon information they had received, detectives discovered that it was either a complete
red herring, a genuine mistake or a case of misidentification, all of which
are inevitable corollaries of a major inquiry.

For example, the day after Susan Maxwell's body had been found,
police were told of a maroon Triumph 2000 motor car that had been
parked near the scene of the abduction with a girl roughly Susan's age
apparently struggling with a man inside the vehicle. Nearly 20,000
owners of maroon Triumph 2000s were traced and interviewed, but the
lead led nowhere.

Police were subsequently criticised for not having revealed that nearby
had been a white van similar to one Black had used when he had been
employed by Poster Dispatch and Storage. Why suggest the white van?
There were surely dozens of vehicles in the vicinity at the time of Susan
Maxwell's abduction; no reason to single out the van for special treatment as the police were unaware at that time that Robert Black was the
man they were seeking.

Some reporters appear to have been obsessed with the apparent relevance of the white van, asking why inquiries had not been made at companies in the vicinity of the abductions to find out if such a vehicle had
delivered on the same day, the assumption being that the inquiries would
have revealed that Black had invariably been nearby on the days that the
children were taken. Such a hypothesis would not have stood up in the
Susan Maxwell case; she had been snatched on a busy country road, away
from the built-up area. In any event Black was not in the habit of calling
at premises in Coldstream, the nearest town to the abduction scene.

Again, with the cases of Caroline Hogg, Sarah Harper and Teresa
Thornhill, Black was later known to have called at firms in Portobello,
Morley and Nottingham prior to abducting, or attempting to abduct, his
victims, but at the time the likelihood of tracing a lone driver who had
relatively minor sex convictions dating back several years from among the
scores who had called at dozens of nearby commercial premises on the
day in question was extremely remote, and could effectively be dismissed.
Police pointed out that with close to 700,000 Transit vans to check nationwide, the task would have been impractical, as well as beyond their
resources.

Others have suggested that Black should have been picked up at the
time following his identification at or near the scene of the abductions.
Such criticism ignores the problems attendant upon the arrest of a

suspect on evidence of identification. These have been well documented; any number of witnesses will provide varying descriptions, all corresponding to a greater or lesser degree. In the case of Robert Black a police artist drew likenesses of the suspect, working from witnesses' descriptions. These impressions bore a remarkable resemblance to Black, but it is unusual for anyone to be traced as the result of such an initiative.

Mistakes and omissions did occur; the failure of the police in Nottinghamshire to connect the attempted abduction of Teresa Thornhill with the other abductions, despite the fact that two years previously Sarah Harper's body had been found within their jurisdiction, is one example. There were others, but it is nonetheless surprising that in view of the duration, extent and complexity of the inquiry there were not more.

Hector Clark acknowledges that mistakes occurred, and that the press were justified in drawing attention to them. He accepts the criticism and hopes that officers on future murder inquiries may learn and benefit from shortcomings in the Black investigation. What has irked him, however, has been the public airing of differences relating to strategy and tactics by those with whom he worked closely, without their first having discussed the matter with him. Clark declines to enter into discussion over the issues in any detail, insisting that they are internal police matters.

It is nevertheless worth looking briefly at the arguments. The main point of contention was that raised by Detective Superintendent John Stainthorpe of the West Yorkshire Police. Stainthorpe had effectively been the officer in charge of the Sarah Harper investigation, and therefore had not become involved in the overall inquiry until 1986, by which time Hector Clark had been heading the Maxwell and Hogg inquiries since the summer of 1982.

Stainthorpe's criticism is that Robert Black's conviction in 1967 for indecent assault, regarded as a relatively minor offence, would nonetheless have come to light had Hector Clark's trawl back through known sex offenders not been confined to serious offences including attempted murder, rape and abduction. The Yorkshire detective went on to argue that had Black's 1967 conviction been recorded at West Yorkshire, he would have been a category 'A' suspect and would soon have come to notice.

From the point of view of Hector Clark, Black was not on West Yorkshire's records but on those of the police in Scotland where his early convictions did not warrant him being regarded as a high risk sexual offender. Clark had necessarily to draw up parameters for the trawl through the records of sex offenders; in view of the nature of the crimes he was investigating, the obvious boundary was to seek out men with major sex convictions. To have included all those with minor convictions with a sexual constituent would have rendered the search unmanageable. Furthermore if it had not gone back fifteen years to 1967, Black's name would still not have emerged.

John Stainthorpe's confidence in saying that Robert Black's name would have appeared on a search through West Yorkshire records is justified: a trawl through the records of one force is a far more straightforward task, and can probe further, than one that extends nationwide.

Hector Clark and John Stainthorpe were both vastly experienced detectives. There is no doubt that Stainthorpe's approach to and management of the inquiry would have varied from Clark's. The Yorkshireman had his own ideas and would have introduced his own initiatives. Whether his strategy would have succeeded in bringing Black's homicidal career to an end sooner than had that of Hector Clark is an open question.

Both men were united in their determination to bring the paedophiliac killer to justice; their differences over the strategy that should have been adopted were largely inconsequential. Perhaps the debate was best summed up by Hector Clark when it was all over: 'The thing that struck me most was the dedication of every police officer involved from Lothian and Borders, Northumbria, West Yorkshire, Staffordshire, Nottinghamshire and Leicestershire to discover and prove who killed these three beautiful little girls.'

The parents of Susan Maxwell, Caroline Hogg and Sarah Harper would surely have endorsed that accolade.

For his trial Robert Black had been transferred from Peterhead to Durham Prison from where he was transported daily under a strong police escort to and from Newcastle Crown Court.

At Peterhead he had been settled in, serving the life sentence imposed in 1990 for the offences involving Mandy Wilson at Stow. The Scottish prison, offering special therapy designed to probe into a sex offender's behaviour, is also a safer physical environment for such men with inmates being at less risk of attack by their fellows than in more conventional prisons. At these, sex offenders are almost invariably segregated for their own safety under Rule 43.

Instead of returning to Peterhead following his conviction, Black was taken from the court to one of six dispersal prisons in England (probably HMP Nottingham), there to await allocation to a more permanent establishment. Despite the Home Office (Prisoner Location Service) being bound by the restrictions of the 1984 Data Protection Act, I have been able to establish that Robert Black was later classified as a category 'A' prisoner and is currently in the segregation unit of the top security prison at Wakefield.

It is likely that at some time his security category will be revised, and that he will be permitted to apply for a transfer back to Peterhead. Apart from being at less physical risk, he will there live a less restricted daily routine.

With Robert Black safely locked away, in all probability for the remainder of his natural life, the door closes on the activities of one of the most cunning, ruthless and depraved child predators ever to have stalked the land.

However, there are others, as yet undetected. Rarely does a week or month pass without there being news of a child sexual abuser being apprehended, a paedophile ring being broken up or a child being reported missing, later to be found dead. There are some who argue that all this is a post-war phenomenon; that affluence conjointly with poverty, unemployment, family break-ups and increasing permissiveness leading to promiscuity, have all contributed to an increase in the number of physical and sexual assaults.

Does this stand up to close examination? During the Victorian era and the early part of the twentieth century the exploitation of children pervaded society. Children, some as young as nine or ten years, worked twelve hours a day in factories and on farms, and in the homes of the wealthy and the aristocracy, as well as errand boys (or girls), bootblacks and at a variety of other menial tasks, to earn a few coppers to bolster the slender finances of a poverty-stricken family. Physical punishment was administered arbitrarily on the slightest pretext, particularly in working class households where large families living in close proximity frequently argued, and sometimes fought with each other.

There is little reason therefore to believe that sexual abuse and attacks on children were less prevalent in that age than now. Formal sex education was non-existent; the facts of life were disseminated among schoolfellows having been passed on by elder brothers or sisters, by observation – there was little privacy in slum dwellings – or, rarely, by

Sunday school teachers. In view of this there would surely have been those prepared to take advantage of such ignorance and naivety to prey on children. The activities of these predators received less publicity than in recent times, people generally remaining unaware and ignorant of their behaviour.

There is no room for complacency; despite educating and warning the young to be ever watchful and on their guard, treating and counselling offenders and awakening the public to the risk, sexual abuse and exploitation of children will, I fear, continue. Occasionally it will escalate into extreme violence, and more rarely murder, when the issues will again come to the fore. Sociologists and penologists will add their voices to those of psychiatrists, newspaper columnists, policemen and members of the public in advancing theories and suggesting remedies from across the penal spectrum to stem the trend.

Perhaps the most chillingly authoritative words of advice were those spoken by Robert Black himself when asked how parents can best protect their children from such as he: 'Never take their eyes off their kids, I suppose,' he replied.

CHAPTER 16

WHERE NEXT?

As Robert Black contemplated spending the rest of his life in prison, detectives turned their attention to a number of other unsolved cases. During the preceding twenty-five years several young schoolgirls had disappeared without trace, most of whom were never to be seen alive again. Parents and families were left to mourn daughters who, by 1994, they could only assume were dead.

Nevertheless, with the dedication that had characterised the Robert Black inquiry, detectives were determined to solve the outstanding cases. Several bore Robert Black's hallmark, so early in their continuing inquiries the policemen considered interviewing him in prison. However, when Black let it be known that he would not co-operate with them, the idea was deferred, perhaps to be revived later.

In the meantime a meeting was convened at which senior detectives involved in the Maxwell, Hogg and Harper inquiries were joined by those from Devon and Cornwall, Hampshire, the Royal Ulster Constabulary and other forces with outstanding inquiries of a similar nature. The meeting was held in July 1994 and took place in the Central police station in Newcastle upon Tyne. Its terms of reference were to look carefully at the evidence that had emerged at Black's trial and in the light of this consider the possibility of his having abducted and killed other children.

There were several cases worth pursuing but two of them had attracted considerable publicity at the time, and many years after the event were still occasionally resurrected in the public's mind.

April Fabb, a pretty thirteen-year-old who lived with her parents and older sisters in the Norfolk village of Metton near Cromer, disappeared on the warm, sunny afternoon of Tuesday, 8 April 1969. She had set out from home to cycle the two miles along a country road to the village of Roughton where her sister Pamela lived with her husband Bernard, a

Cromer electrician. In April's saddlebag were a packet of cigarettes and some handkerchiefs, a present for her brother-in-law on his birthday. April was last seen by a young friend to whom she spoke briefly before continuing. Later that afternoon her discarded bicycle was spotted in a field by a passing motorist. The saddlebag still contained the cigarettes and handkerchiefs, but of April there was no sign.

A massive police search was mounted headed by Chief Superintendent Ronald Lester, the head of Norfolk CID, but despite the unremitting efforts of police and civilians during the spring and summer of 1969, April Fabb was never seen again.

Although there were parallels with the Maxwell, Hogg and Harper cases – the victim was a schoolgirl, she vanished in broad daylight, and she had almost certainly been carried off in a motor vehicle – there were other considerations that made Robert Black's involvement seem less feasible. He had only moved south the previous year, and during the time he had been living in London had worked locally doing casual jobs. Although he may have acquired a vehicle, is it likely that he would have driven nearly one hundred miles to a remote spot in north Norfolk purely on spec?

In the case of Genette Tate, a thirteen-year-old Devon schoolgirl who vanished on Saturday, 19 August 1978 while on her paper round – which she had only commenced the day before – the likelihood that Robert Black was implicated is greater. It was overcast when Genette set out at about 3 p.m. from her home village of Aylesbeare near Exeter, to deliver newspapers to a number of surrounding farms. Shortly afterwards she stopped for a few minutes and chatted to two young girlfriends. Soon after Genette had left them to continue with her round, these two cycled slowly down the lane their friend had taken.

About a quarter of a mile further on they were surprised and alarmed to come across Genette's bicycle lying in the middle of the lane with the newspapers strewn around. Of Genette there was no sign.

Again police and local people joined in a lengthy but fruitless search of the surrounding countryside, assisted by a helicopter from RAF Chivenor, together with police dog handlers and underwater search teams. No trace of the missing girl was found.

At a press conference Acting Chief Superintendent Eric Rundle, the deputy head of Devon and Cornwall CID, who was in charge of the investigation, spoke of 'points of similarity between this case and the unsolved disappearance of a Norfolk schoolgirl, April Fabb, at Metton near Cromer, nine years ago'.

At the time of Genette Tate's disappearance in August 1978, Robert Black was working for Poster Dispatch and Storage. He had been employed by the company for two years and was still delivering posters mainly in the south and south-west of England.

Several detectives are still strongly of the opinion that Robert Black was responsible for Genette Tate's disappearance. Ex-Detective Superintendent John Stainthorpe for one puts the likelihood of his involvement at around 80 per cent.

Another indication that Black was involved in the West Country girl's disappearance had emerged during one of his interviews with Ray Wyre in which he had displayed considerable insight into the abductor's reasoning. Black's remarks had certainly not amounted to a confession, but having been expressed more than twelve years after the event, they had suggested more than a casual interest in the case.

Also discussed at the Newcastle conference was the disappearance of several other young females during the years following Robert Black's arrival in England. It was possible that some of them could be attributed to Black, and after the conference had ended detectives returned to their offices, retrieved the files on outstanding missing and murdered girls and scrutinised again the information that had already been gathered during the inquiries. With their recently acquired knowledge, they hoped that new light would be thrown on these investigations, and that further lines of inquiry would suggest themselves.

It transpired that there were a number of missing person and homicide inquiries the circumstances of which suggested Robert Black's possible involvement. In 1973 he had been living in London for five years but was still not working for PDS. On Monday, 21 May that year, nine-year-old Christine Markham failed to arrive at her school in Scunthorpe. Unlike April Fabb and Genette Tate, Christine vanished from an urban area during the morning rush hour. It seemed inconceivable that her abduction should have passed unnoticed, but despite the usual widespread search and inquiries, Christine was neither seen nor heard of again. This lack of success was even more frustrating for the police than it had been in the Fabb and Tate investigations in view of the lack of response from potential witnesses.

The bodies were found in the cases of Pat Morris, fourteen, a schoolgirl, and Colette Aram, a sixteen-year-old trainee hairdresser. Pat Morris was found on Hounslow Heath, just 400 yards from home on Wednesday, 18 June 1980. She had been strangled. Colette Aram was abducted while on the way to meet friends in November 1983, from Keyworth, south of Nottingham. Her half-naked body was discovered later in a field where she had been raped and strangled.

There are others: Suzanne Lawrence, a fourteen-year-old who vanished from Harold Hill, Essex, in 1969, Marion Crofts who went missing at Farnborough, Hampshire, on 6 June 1981, and Lisa Hession, another fourteen-year-old Manchester schoolgirl who disappeared on 9 December 1984. All these cases came up for discussion at the July 1994 meeting of senior CID officers, and inquiries were subsequently reopened in different parts of the United Kingdom. These are continuing.

Police forces in the United Kingdom are not the only ones with similar cases outstanding. Detectives from France, Holland and Germany had also hoped to interview Robert Black following his conviction, but like their British counterparts they were to be frustrated by his refusal to co-operate.

The French police were most interested in Robert Black's Continental journeyings. During the summer of 1987, four nine-year-old girls were abducted and strangled, three of them after having been raped. The attacks all took place near Paris. Virgine Delmas was taken on 9 May 1987, while on her way to the shops in a northern suburb. Three weeks later on 30 May, Perrine Vigneron was abducted from Bouleurs, an eastern suburb, while on her way to a pottery class; her body was found six weeks later a few miles away at Chelles. The spate of child abductions continued on 3 June, at Malakoff, on Paris's southern outskirts, when the body of Helma Greendahry was discovered. Finally, on 27 June, at Bievres, south-west of the capital, Sabine Dumont was abducted soon after a white Transit van was later reported to have been seen in the vicinity; her body was found nearby the following day.

The time span encompassing these four crimes, and the similar *modus operandi*, suggested that they were the work of an individual who lived or worked in or near Paris, or who periodically visited the city; Black could well have come within the latter category.

The French authorities were also anxious to speak to Black regarding three other unsolved child murders that had occurred during the 1980s elsewhere in the country. The Gendarmerie were aware that Black stayed in a caravan in the Dordogne region when visiting Eddie and Kathy Rayson at their home outside Toutoirac. The French police were seeking to establish whether Black had been in France, and if so where, at the time the children were abducted.

Similarly, the Dutch police, knowing of the trips Robert Black had made to Amsterdam to add to his collection of pornography, wished to question him about the unsolved killing of Cheryl Marien, a seven-year-old who disappeared from Velsen near Amsterdam in August 1986.

German detectives also joined the queue to interview Black, and detectives from the Royal Ulster Constabulary were anxious to ask him about two children who had gone missing from County Antrim. All these inquiries are being held in abeyance in the hope that at some time in the future Robert Black will change his mind and decide to answer questions and co-operate with the various criminal investigation departments.

Meanwhile a team of Lothian and Borders detectives headed by Detective Chief Inspector Roger Orr have been liaising through Interpol with their Continental colleagues to try to establish whether or not, with the information already to hand, there is anything to link Robert Black with their outstanding inquiries. He has been eliminated from involvement in some of the cases as he was at home in England at the relevant times. Joint investigation into others is continuing.

Similarly at home; armed with the fresh information that emerged at Black's trial, detectives throughout the country are actively pursuing resurrected inquiries that have lain dormant for several years. They are as dedicated as were their predecessors to solving these crimes. Whether or not any of them will eventually be attributed to Robert Black remains to be seen. Meanwhile the grief, sadness and horror that assailed the Maxwell, Hogg and Harper families for so long were assuaged somewhat when Robert Black, one of the most evil and dangerous child predators of modern times, was locked away.

Only memories remain.

APPENDIX

List of charges to which Robert Black pleaded not guilty at Newcastle Crown Court, on Wednesday, 13 April, 1994.

1. That on July 30, 1982, at Cornhill-on-Tweed in the county of Northumberland he did unlawfully and by force or fraud kidnap Suzan Claire Maxwell against her will, contrary to common law;

2. Between July 29, 1982 and August 13, 1982, at or near Loxley, Uttoxeter, Staffordshire, or elsewhere in England and Wales, did murder Suzanne Claire Maxwell, contrary to common law;

3. Between July 29, 1982 and August 13, 1982, at or near Loxley, Uttoxeter, without lawful excuse prevented the proper burial of a dead body, namely that of Suzanne Claire Maxwell;

4. Between July 7 and 19, 1983, in various places in England and Wales did unlawfully and injuriously falsely imprison Caroline Hogg and detain her against her will;

5. Between July 7 and 19, 1983, at or near Twycross, Leicestershire, or elsewhere in England and Wales, did murder Caroline Hogg, contrary to common law;

6. Between July 7 and 19, 1983, at or near Twycross, Leicestershire, without lawful excuse did prevent the proper burial of a dead body, namely that of Caroline Hogg;

7. On March 26, 1986, at Morley, West Yorkshire, unlawfully or by

force or by fraud did take or carry away Sarah Jane Harper against her will;

8. Between March 25, 1986, and April 20, 1986, at or near Radcliffe on Soar, Nottinghamshire, or elsewhere in England and Wales, did murder Sarah Jane Harper, contrary to common law;

9. Between March 28, 1986, and April 20, 1986, at or near Radcliffe on Soar, Notts, or elsewhere without lawful excuse did prevent the proper burial of a dead body, namely that of Sarah Jane Harper;

10. On April 24, 1988, at Radford, Nottingham, Nottinghamshire, did kidnap Teresa Ann Thornhill against her will, contrary to common law.

BIBLIOGRAPHY

CLARK, HECTOR, with JOHNSTON, DAVID, *Fear the Stranger*, Mainstream Publishing, 1994.

WYRE, RAY, and TATE, TIM, *The Murder of Childhood*, Penguin Books, 1995.

FAIRWEATHER, BARBARA, *A Short History of Kinlochleven*, Glencoe and North Lorn Folk Museum, 1985.